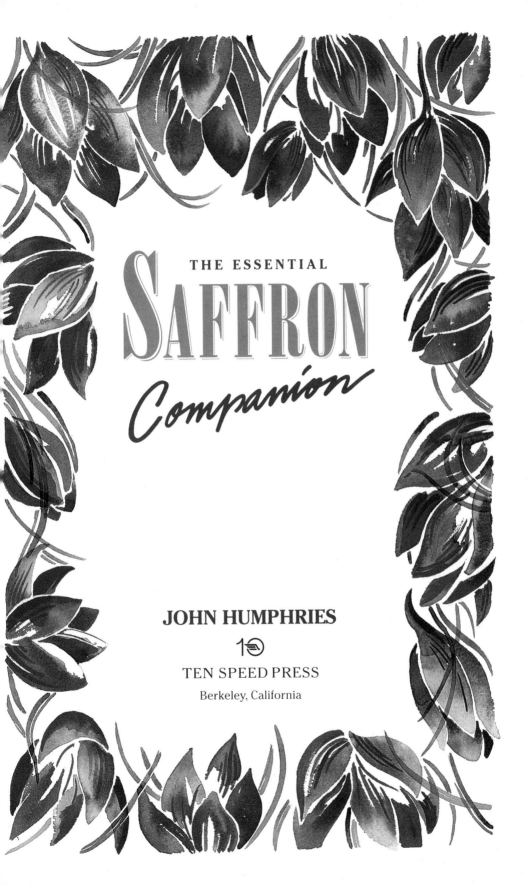

THE ESSENTIAL

SAFFRON
Companion

JOHN HUMPHRIES

TEN SPEED PRESS

Berkeley, California

1🖾

Ten Speed Press
Box 7123
Berkeley, California 94707
www.tenspeed. com

Distributed in Australia by Simon & Schuster
Australia, in Canada by Ten Speed Press
Canada, in New Zealand by Tandem Press,
in South Africa by Real Books, in Singapore,
Malasia, and Indonesia by Berkeley Books,
and in the United Kingdom and Europe
by Airlift Books.

Designed and formatted by
Adam Denchfield Design
Illustrations by Madeleine David
Color origination by Modern Age Repro

Library of Congress Cataloging-in-Publication
Data on file with publisher.

Printed in Italy

First Ten Speed printing, 1998

1 2 3 4 5 6 7 8 9 10—02 01 00 99 98

*For Sylvia, Harry, and Kate, in
memory of the two Maggies and for
hunter-gatherers everywhere*

CONTENTS

ACKNOWLEDGMENTS

A golden contribution was made by the following. Many thanks to you all.

Jeannette Lee, Gordon and Franca Vinnicombe, David Eyre, Mike Belben, Mark Yates, Tim and Linda Shepherd, Steve and Rosie Bull, Norman and Sue Lomax, Neil and Sue Floyd, Bill Miller, Jake and Debbie Behnan, Mark and Mandi Opee, Joseph Behnan, Bina Lay, Sister Mary Murphy, James and Sheridan Walton, Jon Spiteri, Trevor Gulliver, Vivian, Merele Murphy, Mike and Juliet Graham, E Corrett. Russell Cronin, George Dorgan, Tom and Frances Bissell, Michael Bateman, Michael Jackson, Lynda Brown. Derek Cooper, Fiona Beckett, Michael Raffael, Maria Jose Sevilla, John and Caroline Riden, Mrs P Warburg, Maureen Evans, Heather Coppock, Carl Anderson, Lucy Gush, Jane Send, Allison Draper, Malcolm Stuart, Emma Walker, Jette Seward, Peo Cederlof, Luis Gonzales, Luz Gonzales, Sylvia Adolpound, Adolf and Montse Viadiu, Jordi Zena, Felix Martinez, Mr. and Mrs. Mahalingan, Mrs Hilary Pristley, Graham Pike, Kit Norman, Patrick Rothan, Liz Day, Anne Croker, Frankie Cole, Mary Griffiths, Mrs J Rowlands, Edwina Simpson, David Bateson, Andrew Tozer, Martin Forsyth, Alan Gregory, Kristina Giernat Boon, Lucy Hall, Patricia Langton, Vicky Hayward, Alice Seferiades, Jane Marsden, Andy Brook, Clive Patten, Anne Dolamore, and John Davies.

Ellen Szita for getting me interested and Kate, my wife, for her support.

Frances Bissell for her foreword.

Thank you to the following companies, publications, and organizations for providing help and information:

Sharwoods, Schwartz, Overseal Natural Ingredients, J Sainsbury, Tesco, Barts Spices, Baldwins Herbs, Boots, Safinter S.A., Jamex & Co, Perfection Foods, Fox's Spices, L Aquila, The ISO Geneva, MAFF, Maison Caurette, Laurent Perrier, Telcher Bros, John E Fells & Sons, *Spain Gourmetour*, *Country Living Magazine*, *Gardens Illustrated*, *Independent on Sunday*, *The Times*, *Sunday Times*, British Pepper and Spice, Unbar Rothan Ltd., Lion Foods, Spanish Chamber of Commerce, Foods from Spain, ICEX, Odysea Ltd., Brindisa, Tapador, ABC Worldwide UK, The Bank of England, Green Cuisine, Cambridge Physic Garden, Plougheath Ltd., The Tate Gallery, The Royal Academy, Sainsbury Wing of the National Gallery, Wings.

Translators:

Spanish	Jainne Gilson
Catalan	Cristina Ruiz
French	Maria Sparling
Swedish	Katrin Olander

Word Processing:

Many thanks to Chris Springham and Jean Sloots of Kwik Kopy, London SE24 and especially Claire Butler of Grub Street.

Chefs:

Rowley Leigh, Alastair Little, David Eyre, Amanda Prichett, Adam Robinson, Simon Hopkinson, Fergus Henderson, Rick Stein, Joyce Molyneux, Ian Ellison, Gunther Schlender, Cathy Gradwell.

FOREWORD

It is summer as I read that Nicholas Culpeper, apprenticed to the apothecary at Cambridge University in the 17th century, wrote of saffron, in those days cultivated locally: "It is a herb of the sun, and under the lion, and therefore you need not demand a reason why it strengthens the heart so exceedingly." And I suppose, born under the sign of Leo, I need not demand a reason why saffron is one of my favorite spices. But saffron is a spice for all seasons, as John Humphries readily demonstrates.

One of the things I especially like about *The Essential Saffron Companion* is the author's enthusiasm for his subject. Not content merely to sell it, he set out some years ago to find out all about saffron and to experiment. His description of the "Mancha martini" made me want to go out and buy a bottle of gin to try it for myself. And one gray, dark winter Sunday afternoon, he invited my husband, Tom, and me to his flat for a late lunch. When we entered, we saw that the whole place was bathed in a warm, sunny light, as he had been dyeing all his tablecloths with saffron.

I have used saffron from many parts of the world, including a precious store, bought in Marrakesh from the king's own spice merchant in the spice souk. But, like John Humphries, I became converted to saffron from La Mancha. In the late 1980s a visit to Spain took me through the "celaminas," the saffron gardens of central Spain, and this brought about a chance meeting with one of the growers. He delivered to me a jar containing 14 grams of saffron, which is almost more than one can possibly need.

Saffron is costly because it is labor-intensive, but not, on the scale of things, expensive, and certainly not as expensive as it used to be. In 1812, when the local merchants were supplying the Spanish market in the Caribbean, the Philadelphia commodity exchange listed saffron as being literally worth its weight in gold, quoting one pound of saffron to one pound of gold. John Humphries visited the saffron harvest in La Mancha, and he describes in vivid detail exactly why it takes the stigmas of many thousands of flowers to produce just a small quantity of saffron. One 4-gram box will happily see you through many, many saffron recipes—a modest amount for such culinary reward.

In *The Essential Saffron Companion* the author provides a wealth of saffron recipes: traditional ones from Persia, India, Italy, the south of France, Scandinavia, and Spain—all countries where saffron has always been used as a spice

7

and as a colorant. There too are recipes collected from his contemporaries in modern English cooking, and indeed recipes derived from his own considerable skills as a cook.

The experienced cook will find much inspiration from the chapter on culinary practice, in which John Humphries describes how best to make a saffron infusion, to make the most of its color and flavor, and the relative merits of whole and powdered stigmas. He also suggests interesting ways in which one might use saffron, not restricting himself only to its culinary uses. He looks at it as a coloring matter and at its far less noble imitators. Then too, there is an important chapter on the medicinal uses of saffron, in which its historical role is examined as well as current experiments into its possible uses in the treatment and management of some of today's diseases.

The Essential Saffron Companion sets out to celebrate, explain, and demystify saffron, and it succeeds handsomely. A gap on the bookshelf is now filled by this glowing volume.

Frances Bissell, 1996

INTRODUCTION

The fraternity of saffron merchants pre-dates the Bible. I became the latest recruit in January 1991, a time of deep snow in London and with the Gulf War dominating the world's attention. It was also the depth of Britain's worst economic recession in living memory when I chose to embark on trading the most expensive and precious spice known to man.

An old friend, Rowley Leigh, the head chef of Kensington Place, suggested that I introduce saffron to my company's range of products, as he was experiencing problems with his suppliers. At that time I was importing olive oil, honey, and wines from Spain. Borges, my oil supplier, told me about Safinter S.A., who are based in Barcelona and one of the principal exporters of Spanish saffron. A week later, after an exchange of faxes, my first consignment of saffron was on its way. A modest order of ten 25-gram boxes and ten 4-gram boxes of Mancha Superior saffron filaments—the highest quality saffron in the world, as I was soon to discover.

When, in a few days, the parcel arrived in my office, I was intrigued by the fragrant aroma that surrounded it. As I opened the parcel, a rich, deep, complex scent greeted me, emanating from the plastic boxes containing the dried red stigmas of *crocus sativus*.

Accompanying the saffron were some informational brochures. I read the fascinating story of the saffron trade and the crocus harvest as the air in my office filled increasingly with an earthy, smoky essence, deeply pungent and tenacious. I took a small box home that evening determined to use it to make supper.

But what and how? What quantity of saffron should I use? A quick thumb through some of my cookery books left me only a little wiser. I decided on a saffron rice dish. I cooked the rice in my normal way, one measure of rice to two of water, then added a "pinch" of saffron for the last few minutes of cooking time. It did not produce the bright yellow rice I was expecting, but I experienced two new sensations: an aroma permeated not only the rice but my entire kitchen and an intense flavor, appetizing and familiar, which recalled my childhood.

But saffron makes rice yellow? My ignorance was further compounded when, in a moment of inspiration, I poured some boiling water over a further "pinch" of saffron. The color of liquid slowly became a deep orange, almost red—certainly not yellow. There was an alchemy at work of which I was innocent. I realized I knew very little about this strange substance. Is saffron a herb, or is it a spice? What was Rowley using saffron for? What were its virtues and how was it best used? I had never been so challenged by an ingredient before.

My first day as a saffron trader left me a little bemused and with a host of questions I set about answering. By the summer of 1993, I realized a book was needed. I had discovered much about saffron but I had come to see that it was misunderstood by domestic cooks and some professional chefs. The extent of many people's know-ledge was "yellow" and "expensive," neither of which is necessarily correct. With so much disinformation, hearsay, and myth, this was not surprising. The purpose of this book is to clear the fog and allow you to use saffron, the most aristocratic spice, with knowledge and confidence.

JOHN HUMPHRIES

WHAT IS
SAFFRON?

"It is an herb of the Sun, and under the Lion. Not above ten grains must be given at one time; a cordial if taken in an immoderate quantity, hurts the heart instead of helping it. It quickens the brain; helps consumptions of the lungs, and difficulty of breathing, it is excellent in epidemical diseases, as pestilence, smallpox, and measles. It is a notably expulsive medicine, and a good remedy in the yellow-jaundice. It is a useful aromatic, of a strong penetrating smell, and a warm, pungent, bitterish taste. It is said to be more cordial, and exhilarating than any of the other aromatics, and is particularly serviceable in disorders of the breast in female obstructions, and hysteric depressions. Saffron is endowed with great virtues, for it refreshes the spirits, and is good against fainting-fits and the palpitation of the heart; it strengthens the stomach, helps digestion, cleanses the lungs and is good in coughs. It is said to open obstructions of the viscera, and is good in hysteric disorders. However, the use of it ought to be moderate and reasonable; for when the dose is too large, it produces a heaviness of the head and sleepiness; some have fallen into an immoderate convulsive laughter, which ended in death. A few grains of this is commonly a dose, though some have prescribed it from half a scruple to a scruple and a half."
FROM CULPEPER'S *COMPLETE HERBAL* (A.D. 1653)

SAFFRON is the name given to the three dried, red-colored stigmas (*stigmata*) and part of the white style to which they are attached of *crocus sativus linnaeus*. It is a cultivated, autumn-blooming, purple-flowered crocus, a member of the Iris family (*iridaceace*). The dried stigmas are known as filaments or threads; they must be rehydrated or powdered before use to release all the properties they contain. Saffron's history is extraordinarily long, its precise origin unknown or lost before the dawn of recorded history. It is exuberant, valuable, and complex—one of our oldest culinary companions, it is possibly the first spice ever used by man.

I have a good friend who always keeps a few filaments in a little open dish in her larder. She loves the appetite-provoking aroma that permeates her storeroom, evoking happy memories of feasts, good friends and relaxing holidays. For her, saffron's most treasured attribute is *safranal*, the pungent, tenacious aroma. Audacious or subtle, the earthy bittersweet flavor (*picrocrocin*) of saffron enhances the world's cuisines, in a vast array of cherished recipes and

often festive foods. Although it has been dubbed such grand names as the empress of spices, to pepper's king, it is at this point that the word "spice" fails saffron. And for many other cooks, saffron's principal function is to color (*crocin*) food with the radiance of sunlight. It is this trinity of actions, as an aromatic, a flavoring agent, and a colorant,that distinguishes saffron from other ingredients.

Yet this is only a part of saffron's repertoire; occasionally called a herb, it is in fact a food, as surprisingly, saffron also has a nutritive value, being one of the richest sources of Riboflavin and Vitamin B2. Modern analysis has revealed many of the mysteries of its composition: a rich diversity of proven health-promoting nutrients. Its beneficial influence was noted by the earliest medical practitioners and saffron's use as a remedial agent continues to the present day, its efficacy being confirmed by recent medical research. Saffron is still to be found in recently patented medicines. It is also used by the cosmetic and perfume industries and in the distillation of alchoholic liqueurs. Cleopatra used a saffron wash to keep her skin clear and free from blemishes, and I have also found several references to the plumage of canaries being improved by the addition of a few drops of saffron to their drinking water.

Perhaps the most unusual use of saffron I have encountered, however, is to be found in Laura Esquivel's compelling tale, *Like Water for Chocolate*, set in revolutionary Mexico at the turn of the 20th century. In the book, Tital helps John to make matches (*cerillas*) by coloring the cardboard sticks with saffron before applying the phosphorous mixture!

ITS NAME AND ORIGIN

The two words **saffron** and **crocus**, together with their derivative forms, are recognizable in nearly every language ever spoken by man. Such universal usage is unprecedented and indicates the extreme antiquity of their origin. They share a common resonance that has survived in near identical form since their inception,which echoes from the Bronze Age. This is surely a remarkable dual coincidence perhaps unparalleled in the spheres of botany and etymology. No other commodity or plant has maintained its name, its identity, or its integrity so comprehensively as saffron and the purple crocus that produces it.

Crocus is the older word of the two; its source is believed to be in the Semitic tongue spoken by the peoples who created the first civilizations of the Near and Middle East, including the Nile Delta around 5000 B.C. Saffron probably comes originally from the Sumerian tribes of the Middle East, evolving via the Arabic word *sahafarn* meaning thread and *za'faran* meaning yellow.

Kunkuma is an early Persian word found in the Zend texts and is also found in Sanskrit, the oldest known script of the Indo-European group of languages. Sanskrit records the early Hindu period in the Indus Valley on the western borders of India. The region traded with and was conquered by the pre-classical Persians. It was probably at this time that cultivations of *Kongs* commenced in Kashmir. A later Arabic root is apparent in the old Chinese words of *si-fa-lang* and *tsa-fa-lan*.

Karkom is the Hebrew word found in the poetic and sensual celebration of life we now know as the Song of Solomon in the Old Testament, written one thousand years before Christ. *Kurkama* is found in Syria soon after the Christian era.

Krokhom and *Carcom*, possibly indicating both spice and flower, were spread extensively across the Mediterranean by the Phoenicians who in turn had assimilated Hitte words from a Semitic dialect spoken in Anatolia (Turkey). The Hittes probably introduced the plant into the area, near a town called *Corycus* (*K'pukos*) now Korghoz, where high quality saffron was cultivated for many centuries and was still esteemed by the Romans one thousand years later.

Successive generations of the ancient Greeks were enchanted by *Kpokos* and *Krokos*. There is a town in Macedonia called *Krokos* near *Kozani* where saffron is still cultivated. The modern Greek word for spice is *saphrani*.

Crocum and *Zafaranum* are the Latin words that form the basis of all further derivations having allowed for localized pronunciation and spellings with the exception of Spain, which, because of the Moorish occupation, took the Arabic root in *azafran*.

In Latin, there is a range of related words which describe the many functions of saffron's use in ancient Rome. *Crocórula* and a *crocóta* were the names for a yellow-colored robe worn by women. *Cróco* and *crocatatius* both pertain to dyeing yellow with saffron, a task for a *crocotarii*, a tradesman dyer. *Crocinus* is an all-embracing term and *crocias* a valuable yellow stone, probably amber. *Spica Cilissa* suggests a greater culinary use of saffron at the time of Strabo, who also refers to a *Corycian* product, the saffron grown in Anatolia by the Cilician descendants of the Hittes. A latter-day but nonetheless old Italian word was *zaffrone* and "to *zafferanato* a dish" was to make it yellow.

Saffroune was in use in France at the end of the Dark Ages. In *Liber Coquina*, a French cookery book from the Middle Ages, the words *safranium* and *crocum* are found; the former is believed to mean safflower and the latter real saffron. *Safroun*, *safron* and *safryn* are early English spellings from the medieval period, the word crocus having evolved completely by this time.

It was after the crusades that **Endore** started to appear in English and **Endorée** and *Endorêt* in French. This is a culinary term that specifically indicates the coloring of food yellow (mainly roasts and pastry) with a saffron-based wash. Both the word and the technique are derived from the Persian. "Endore the coffyn (pie) withoute, with saffroun and almond mylke" and "when the endoringe is stiff let them rost no more" are culinary instructions from the 15th century, as is to make a "*jaunette*," a saffron yellow sauce. *Endore* is still to be found in the 1989 edition of the Oxford English Dictionary, published by the Clarendon Press: "To cover with a yellow glaze, of yolk of egg and saffron." Randall Cotgrave's Dictionary of 1611 makes reference to a *saffranier*, a seller of saffron, and *saffrané*, meaning seasoned or colored with saffron.

The Latin prefix of *croco*, indicating the use of saffron for medical purposes, is to be found in the titles of pharmacopoeias and early health manuals. In 1430 in England *Liber cure crocorum* was published and in Scotland the splendidly titled E*mplastrum Oxycroceum*, part of the Edinburgh Pharmacopoeia. The fantastical *Crocologia* by Hertodt was published in Germany in 1670. In a family "herball," dated 1755, *faffron* is found; the "f" was also in use in the 15th century.

Be aware that historical references can interchange spice and flower words.

A similar word may mean safflower or turmeric and on other occasions it is a poetic reference or metaphor for the color yellow only.

It is also interesting to note that, by journeying from the Semitic to the Sanskrit and back via the Arabic, we arrive at a Latin word *curcuma*, now the species name of turmeric, thus sowing the seeds of latter-day confusion.

The word saffron is an international epicurean definition that singularly unites mankind in a way no other cultivated substance ever has. Its nomenclature is more common than the words we use for water. This ultimately suggests one core source of the plant, the spice it bears, and the word we all know it by. Or could it all have been divine intervention, as the ancient Greeks would have us believe?

The Name Worldwide

The Spanish word is *azafran*, the Catalan *safra*, the French *safran*, the Italian *zafferano*, the Portuguese *agafráo*, the Swedish *saffran*, the Finnish *saframi*, the German *saffran*, the Dutch *saffraan*, the Polish *szafrran*, the Hungarian *sáfrány*, the Romanian *safranu*, the Latvian *safrána*, the Armenian *khekhrum*, the Russian *shafran*, the Turkish *zaferen*, the Arabic *záFarán*, the Iranian *kurkum*, the Kashmiri *kongs*, the Tamil *kungumapu*, the Bengali *jafran*, the Hindi *kesar* or *zafran*, the Teluga *kumkum*, the Chinese *fan-nung-hua*, the Japanese *safuran*, the Malay *safárum,* and the Vietnamese *câynghé*.

THE SAFFRON CROCUS

The ancient Greeks thought that the heavenly substance emanated from the love of Krokos for the nymph, Smilax. The gods, tired of their intense courtship, changed Smilax into a yew bush and Krokos, by the power of his love, into the saffron crocus. No love story is complete, however, without a little bloodshed. A further legend describes the death of Krokos while discus throwing with Hermes. Where the boy's blood was spilt, the first saffron crocus grew with blood-red stigmas.

The saffron crocus is sterile and does not propagate by seed. It has to be cultivated, and increases by the division of cormlets (little bulbs) that form around the main corm. It has a much wider range than the wild crocuses from which it is believed to have descended. No other crocus variety has either the long stigmas (up to 1½ inches) or large petals.

Another rare characteristic in a cultivated plant is that specimens collected from around the world are identical, which suggests a common source for the saffron crocus. Although it has been known by several names other than *Crocus Sativus Linnaeus*, all are the same plant.

There has been a great deal of research into the crocus. Over 90 varieties have now been identified. They are native to the eastern Mediterranean, the Balkans, and near East, but none has been found to be indigenous to India, the Himalayas, Arabia, Egypt, Britain, or America.

The cultivated form must have originated in very early times from one or more of the allied wild forms, which are found east of the Adriatic Sea. It is believed to have evolved from either *crocus cartwrightianus*, a native of Greece, or from *crocus nudiflorus*, which is found in Turkey, Greece, Crete, Italy, North Spain, and Malta. This latter variety was brought to the north of England by the Knights of St. John, and naturalized well as it spread itself by use of stolons, a trailing shoot that takes root, as well as by formation of cormlets. It flowers more readily than *crocus sativus* but produces short stigmas of low potency. It is rarely packed as the saffron of commerce. Growing conditions, soil type, soil drainage, harvesting, and drying methods all contribute to the potency of the best qualities.

Saffron is unusual, being a spice produced by the sex organs, albeit sterile, of a flower. The only other "flower spice" of any importance is the clove, which is a whole, dried, partly formed blossom flower of a tropical evergreen tree from the family *Myrtaceae*, that grows up to 39 feet in height. Really, not even close to the same thing.

THE COLOR

An attention-seeking burst of prismatic color heralds the nocturnal birth of *crocus sativus*, with its voluptuous purple-blue petals, chive green leaves, fluffy yellow stamen, and the prized, rage–red stigmas. A floral spectrum, the envy of many other blooms, it takes man's intervention to reveal the plant's colorific treasure. For by a true act of alchemy, red's rage is mellowed and becomes the most perfect golden yellow.

The delicate appearance of saffron belies its energy as a colorant, for concealed within the filigree stigmas is the lionhearted *crocin* (C44 H64 O24), a potent natural dye which in its pure form can color up to 150,000 times its own weight unmistakably yellow. *Crocin* also yields the secondary pigment of saffron, *crocetin*. Crocin is also extracted from the fruits of *Gardenia jasminoides*. Saffron's coloring power is measured as an indicator of quality by the ISO standard (see Appendix III, page 154). For the top quality, category I, the *crocin* content must reach a level of 190; lower categories are considerably less colorful. The most potent I have encountered measure 220 on the same scale. The potential of category I saffron is to color up to 10,000 times its own volume a strong shade of yellow.

Such potency, and the brightness of saffron's light, enraptured our forefathers, whose desire was to harness such a powerful and valuable resource. By cultivating the plant they were able to harvest a dependable crop each autumn, which would illuminate the dark ensuing winter with a beam of sunny yellow.

For the artist, from cave painter to Picasso, saffron's pigment has personified yellow. For the pâtissier, saucier, chef, baker, and food technician, saffron brings the color of the sun to the table. For the textile weaver, saffron was the most versatile, heat stable, water soluble, dye, that added warm tones to carpets, rugs, linen, lace, silk, tweed, shawls, Indian saris, Tudor ruffs, Roman togas, and the bandages of Egyptian mummies. For more than one ancient culture, saffron's particular hue was the color associated with immortality. For the distiller and perfumer, a luminous tint, which by good fortune was also deeply aromatic. For the pharmacist, saffron was used until this century to color medicines; it is therefore surprising to discover it has now been replaced for this purpose by E102 tartrazine and E110 sunset yellow, in a complete reversal of the apothecary's wisdom and art.

Saffron has long been allied with joy and cheerfulness, a charm which made it the celebratory color of bridal dresses in classical Rome and in present-day India, where the dowry of Hindu brides will often contain *kesar*, to elaborate the festive clothing and also to create the intricate wedding day facial and hand colorations. The holy ascetic's use of saffron to mark sacred symbols on their foreheads (a *tillak*) is deliberate, in the belief that the saffron itself, because of its purity and grace, induces a higher spiritual serenity. It was for similar reasons that at the time of Buddha's death, his followers chose saffron-colored robes in an act of enlightened remembrance. The Buddhist monks' use of saffron pigment is surely the most famous and oldest coloring tradition in the world, now spanning 25 centuries.

To the earliest civilizations, saffron was valued as a dye and a colorant of cloth, before any culinary or medical applications. It was as a dye that it became an item of economic importance that was traded and bartered throughout the known world. The carpet weavers of ancient Persia appreciated saffron's primary hue; its ability to mix with and enhance other dye stuffs was equally prized. Extensive cultivation of saffron in Persia was necessary to supply the carpet industry; it was grown from the shores of the Caspian Sea to the Persian Gulf and at the great weaving centers of Khorásán, Isfahan, and Fars. The Phoenicians based at Tyre and Sidon developed a dye-based export economy, and they traded large quantities of saffron and Tyrian purple, an extract of shellfish, across the Mediterranean and beyond.

Saffron also illuminated the classical world and its literature with its benevolent glow. A Greek, Plutarch, states explicitly that before dyeing a cloth with saffron it must first be treated in a bath of alum, as a mordant. The Romans would employ the specialist skills of a *crocotarii*, to bathe togas and wedding veils evenly in a strong saffron solution.

The sheer majesty of saffron's yellow made it the chosen color of royalty from the Pharaohs to the Tudors. Henry VIII ruled that such a regal hue should be the sole preserve of the crown and nobility. He forbade the people of Ireland to use saffron to dye clothing. In doing so, Henry ended a very old Irish tradition of dyeing the cloaks and mantles of their kings with the color that signified their rank. The last vestige of this old Gaelic/Celtic tradition was recorded in the Hebrides in the 18th century.

In pious Ireland, saffron-dyed bed linen was considered beneficial for strengthening the limbs. In passionate Spain, *azafran*-colored bed sheets are considered to be a suitable wedding night extravagance, that would improve love-making and fertility. The Moors taught the Spanish to stain leather with saffron by making a transparent yellow varnish with aloe, linseed oil, and turpentine. The Crusaders returned from the Holy Land with saffron-stained leather prayer strips and book markers. Saffron was also applied to missals, the illuminated medieval manuscripts, as an alternative to gold leaf.

It was in the Middle Ages that saffron was last used to any great extent as a cosmetic colorant in Europe, much to the consternation of Henry II, who feared that there would be none left for the royal table. Like Cleopatra before them, the ladies of court would tint their hair and sheen fingernails, lips, and skin with an attractive lustre, which would have been highlighted by the flickering flames of candles and lamps.

Recently, I was surprised to find a smoked fish product colored with *crocin* in my local supermarket. Investigations revealed that *crocin* has been used by the food processing industry as a natural, if costly alternative to the azo-dyes. Other than coloring smoked fish, *crocin* has been used in flour-based confectionery and dairy products, and in soft drinks and sugar-based confectionery such as the traditional barley sugar and lemon curd. *Crocin* is stable to ascorbic acid and it will help to prevent oxidation of foods. Although *crocin* was listed as a permitted food color in the United Kingdom food regulations of 1973, it has now been revoked. The revoking legislation states that because saffron is also an aromatic (in fact it says this is its primary use!) it can no longer be a permitted food color because coloring is its secondary use. Am I alone in thinking the EU has got this the wrong way round? Saffron's most powerful virtue is its color, and aroma is a further benefit.

I have given a new lease of life to old tablecloths and napkins with the aid of a saffron bath. Being a water soluble dye, it is necessary to use a mordant to fix the yellow. Alum (salts of aluminium and potassium) and cream of tartar are suitable mordants for saffron, but careful use of small quantities of a cold-water solution of stannous chloride (tin) will give the most brilliant yellow.

My method is to use a white plastic bucket which allows you to "see" the color. I then determine the minimum amount of water needed to saturate the cloth. I then color the water with saffron. Sometimes I use powdered saffron, which I boil for five minutes in a liter of water before adding it to the bucket. On other occasions I have used whole filaments, which I leave to infuse in a liter of water for 24 hours or more, before adding to the bucket. Whole filaments will produce "hot spots" of color, which can be quite attractive in themselves.

I first soak the cloth in plain water, then in the mordant solution for a few minutes before placing the cloth in the saffron bath. I will then leave the cloth to soak for an hour. When I remove it, I allow the saffron solution to drain back into the bucket. I then place the cloth in a mordant solution for five minutes and then finally remove and dry it in the shade in the open air. Wash separately the first time to be sure the dye is set. The remaining saffron solution can be retained and bottled in dark glass for other dyeing applications.

To get a strong, vivid yellow from a bucketful of water I will start with 1 gram of saffron. I will then do a color test. I may then add more saffron until I achieve the strength of color I require.

I have also stained wood with a water-based concentrated saffron solution (it highlights the wood grain and looks good in bright sunlight) which when dried I have varnished with a matte polyurethane varnish to protect it.

I also make a saffron ink, to sign Christmas and birthday cards and to write party invitations. For this, I use a sachet of powdered saffron infused with an eggcupful of white alcohol (gin, for example). I leave the infusion for a day or more, which allows it to concentrate itself by evaporation, before filling a fountain pen with the ink to illuminate my correspondence with the most perfect shade of yellow.

SAFFRON THROUGH THE AGES

"Your lips drop sweetness like honeycomb my bride, syrup and milk are under your tongue, and your dress has the scent of Lebanon, Your cheeks are an orchard of pomegranates, an orchard full of rare fruits, spikenard and saffron, sweet cane and cinnamon."

SONG OF SOLOMON (1000 B.C.)

I CAN ONLY speculate as to how saffron's original seduction of mankind came about. Could it be that our distant forefathers were attracted to the plant by the beauty of the purple flowers that appeared overnight, at an unusual time of the year? When the flowers were examined more closely, were their fingers stained bright yellow, by the wet, fresh, red stigmas of a wild crocus? Dye stuffs, after all, were of huge importance to early people and became one of the first commodities traded. Left in the sun for a day or two was a small pile of stigmas inadvertently dried? The resultant compelling aroma perhaps attracted further investigation and use.

Pollen samples found in caves in Iraq, occupied by man 50,000 years ago, indicate the use of many wild plants. Wild crocus stigmas could have been used for their pigment by early cave painters.

Ancient man was enamored and sought to have a dependable supply. Consequently, the saffron crocus were cultivated in this area for some 7,000 years. However, the true location of the origin of the saffron crocus is lost before the dawn of recorded history.

Wild crocus plants are native to the eastern Mediterranean, the Balkans and Near East. Saffron is one of the few spices not to originate in India or the Tropics and is very probably the first spice ever used by man. Various locations for the first sites of cultivation have been suggested. Most fall into the wide arc known as the Fertile Crescent, where many wild plants we know today as foodstuffs were first cultivated.

Ten thousand years ago in Persia, saffron was a favored natural dye for sheep and goat skins. The ancient Persian carpet industry created a demand for saffron. Cultivation of the saffron crocus has probably been continuous in Iran since these early times. The early Persian civilizations and empires spread its use and cultivation east to the Indus Valley and west to the shores of the Mediterranean.

Other researchers and the people themselves claim Kashmir to be the spiritual home of saffron. Excellent saffron has certainly been cultivated there for several thousand years, as Alexander the Great discovered in 326 B.C., but the crocus is not indigenous to the region so it unlikely that Kashmir is the original site.

In southern Turkey in the region of Cilicia, as I mentioned earlier, there is a town called Corycus (now Korghoz). The obvious similarity of the name to the word "crocus" is self-evident. It is from this region that the great saffron traders, the Phoenicians, were to obtain their supply many centuries later—Cilician saffron was considered to be the best by the Romans.

In Greece there is an ancient town called Krokos in Macedonia near Kozani where saffron is still a yearly cash crop. Saffron soon became a commodity of immense value and importance. Its warm golden hue was associated with the sun, wisdom and spirituality. Its importance was depicted in word and picture of many cultures across many lands throughout the centuries. Dating from some fifteen hundred years B.C. there are surviving frescoes from the Cretan palace of Minos, one depicting a monkey gathering crocus flowers; a later period fresco shows young women harvesting saffron.

The Ebyers Papyrus, the great text of Egyptian medicine (around 1600 B.C.) describes cosmetic applications of saffron to improve the complexion and details of cultivation of the plant in the Luxor Gardens. Even a thousand years before Christ, saffron was becoming a widely traded substance thanks to the Phoenicians, who are said to have been addicted to saffron and traded it even as far as Britain.

Homer, in the *Iliad*, robed Eos, the goddess of dawn, in saffron's brilliant colors. Zeus, the king of the Greek gods is said to have slept on a mattress stuffed with saffron. Dionysus covered Ariadne with a veil of saffron to ensure her immortality.

Several centuries later the Roman Empire further spread the trade in saffron and new cultivation sites for the saffron crocus extended through Spain and into Britain. In the first century A.D., Apicius, the great Roman gourmet, published his *De Re Coquinaria*, which described saffron sauces for fish and fowl and its use in the preparation of wine-based aperitifs.

After the fall of the Roman Empire, very little saffron was used in England. The taste for the spice was re-awakened by the Normans and the returning Crusaders and, as the trade began to expand, supplies became available from the merchants of Genoa and Venice but at a great price. From the household accounts (1265 A.D.) of Eleanor, Countess of Leicester, wife of Simon de Montfort, we discover that saffron cost 10 to 14 shillings a pound, whereas pepper could be had for less than a shilling a pound.

Saffron came to England both from the East, via the Italian Mediterranean ports and from Spain, the major supplier. Distribution was achieved by means of the great fairs of the period. Champagne in France, Mainz in Germany, and Flanders in Belgium were important centers. As was Basel in Switzerland, which adopted the saffron crocus into the city's coat of arms. English merchants traveled in Europe trading wool, linen and tin for spices. Such was the quantity and value of the cargoes of saffron, pepper, ginger, cinnamon, mace, and cloves arriving at the Port of London, that in 1180 the Guild of Peppers was founded to regulate the trade. This was one of the oldest London trade guilds, which in the 14th century incorporated the grossers (grocers) and the apothecaries (chemists).

In 1316 the Pepperers issued a proclamation prohibiting the "anointing with oil or the bathing in water of saffron" in particular and of other spices. An official stamp was affixed to the spice bales, as a guarantee of purity, before they were weighed for sale.

Eight bags of saffron were stolen from Basel in 1374. An army was raised to go in pursuit of the thieves and this led to a "Saffron War."

In 1358 the Safranschau, one of the first food laws, governing the quality and inspection of any saffron offered for sale, was implemented in Nuremberg, Germany, with severe consequences for anyone caught adulterating their merchandise. In 1444 Jobst Findeker of Nuremberg, was found guilty of adulteration of saffron. He was sentenced to be burned at the stake with his impure product. Elss Pfragnerin was buried alive in 1456 in Nuremberg with her "saffron" for a similar offense. Severe consequences indeed. Note that this pre-dates the famous German beer purity law, the Reinheitsgebot, by 158 years.

With royal patronage in France, King Henry II encouraged the cultivation of saffron. He too introduced a quality law, supported by corporal punishment for frauds.

SAFFRON WALDEN

It may be a myth, but a pilgrim is said to have been the founding father of saffron cultivation in England. He returned from the Holy Land to his native Chypping Walden in Essex with a single saffron corm hidden in his hollowed-out staff. It was concealed because the penalty for smuggling such a highly valued commodity out of its home country would have been death. His name is unfortunately lost, but his act of agrarian espionage was said by Hackluyt in 1580 to have occurred in 1339. This solitary corm was to spawn an industry and be the only spice ever cultivated commercially and exported from England. What is certain is that the cultivation of *crocus sativus* commenced and quickly expanded during the long reign of Henry III (1327-1377). The following 400 years of saffron production brought great wealth and fame to the town and a change of name to Saffron Walden by the early 16th century.

The success of the industry has much to do with right place, right time. The local wool merchants created a huge demand for dye-stuffs. A dye-works is mentioned in the Court Rolls of Chypping Walden in 1381. The availability of locally cultivated saffron was of great economic importance to the textile producers, as previously imported saffron was very expensive. Appreciation of the spice was on the increase elsewhere, popularized by the Normans and consolidated by the home-coming crusaders of the 12th and 13th centuries who had developed a taste for the spice while in the Levant. There was also a ready market at court, from the nobility and the church, and an increasing demand for saffron

from the emerging apothecaries. Saffron also became very expensive at a time of plague, as it was considered to be an effective antidote.

There are many references to saffron in the 15th century town records. In 1420 saffron became a taxable commodity. Saffron gardens were bequeathed to sons in wills. The abbott imposed a levy on saffron grown within the abbey precincts. There is an illustration of eight crocus flowers on the spandrels of one arch of the south aisle of Walden's parish church in the diocese of Ely. St. Mary the Virgin was rebuilt between 1450 and 1525, one of the largest in Essex financed in part by the prosperous saffron industry.

The early 16th century saw the zenith of production and the official change of the town's name in a charter granted by Henry VIII in 1514, which was decorated with crocus flowers in the margins. A further charter was granted by Edward VI in 1549. On this, crocus flowers are enclosed by a portcullis and four towers, which became the borough's arms and seal (see illustration on page 25). The town paid tribute with gifts of saffron in ornate casks to royal visitors at nearby Audley End: 14 ounces of saffron (worth £3.11.8d) were presented to Queen Elizabeth I in 1566, Charles II in 1666, William III in 1689, and George I. William III in 1717, and George III received his in a silver goblet.

Camden recorded in 1586 "the field around Walden make a show with this plant, here, on every side smell sweetly and smile pleasantly with saffron." John Norden writing an account of Essex in 1594 describes, "About the town of Walden groweth great store of saffron whose nature in yielding her fruite is verie strange and bindeth the laborer to greate travaile [work] and diligence, and yet at length yealdeth no small advantage to re-comforte him agayne."

During his twenty years as rector of Radwinter (1571–1593), 5 miles from Saffron Walden, the Rev. William Harrison was able to record a firsthand account of saffron production. He states that the crockers (growers) selected land with a chalky soil, more specifically a temperate dry clay on a substratum of chalk, the prime site being the fields on the Cambridge side of Walden. This soil composition is similar to that of La Mancha, Spain. Of growing conditions, Harrison hopes for "warm nights, sweet dews, fat grounds and misty mornings."

Crocus corms were planted in July and harvested in late September. Harrison tells of rising before dawn to complete the harvest by 11 A.M. He says "the floure beginneth to appear of a whitish blue and hath in the middest there of three chives, verie red and pleasant to behold." Wet stigmas were spread on canvas and dried in small kilns before being formed into cakes for sale. At its peak, cultivation of the saffron crocus in Essex and Cambridgeshire extended to the villages of Cherry Hinton, Whittlesford, Duxford, Fulbourn, Chesterford, Littlebury, Ickleton, Hunxton, and colleges at the University. It was also grown in neighboring Suffolk.

The industry suffered various ups and downs despite the efforts of men such as Sir Thomas Smith, who urged the growers to make a greater effort in the late 16th century. At the same time, 1581, Hackluyt implored a friend about to travel to Turkey to see if there could be a market there or in Syria for English saffron. He said, "for if a vent [market] might be found, men in Essex and in Cambridgeshire would revive the trade for the benefit of setting the poore to worke."

Decline set in during the late 17th and early 18th centuries, cheaper fron began to be imported and export markets were lost. Moreover, the formulation of other materials for dye-stuffs hastened its end. By 1726, Littlebury was the only village in the vicinity of Walden producing saffron. *Millers Garden Dictionary* was published in 1768. It informs us of the economics of saffron production in and around Walden at this time. Saffron was sold at 30 shillings (£1.50) a pound. The net profit per acre was around £5, plus any extra income from the sale of surplus corms. Miller recommends rotating the saffron crop with barley.

W. Clark of Shelford, a village near Cambridge, made this interesting observation of imported saffron in 1771 "saffron produced and brought from Spain is greatly inferior to ye English on account of y oylls [oils] the Spaniards use in drying it loose and not pressed cakes as the English do."

By 1790, saffron had disappeared from Walden, and it had to be brought in from Cambridgeshire for the town's fair. The last record of saffron cultivation in the area was by a man named Knott who lived in Duxford and grew a half–acre in 1816.

There have been efforts to reintroduce the saffron crocus into the region in recent times but not on a commercial basis. Maureen Evans at the Saffron Walden museum has not met with much success and claims that rabbits have a great appetite for the corms. Heather Coppock has had more luck in the garden at Cherry Hinton and kindly sent me a sample of her extremely rare English saffron. Corms (bulbs) are available from the Saffron Walden Museum.

Saffron was also grown by the bishops of Ely, in the grounds of the Cathedral in Cambridgeshire and at their palace in London. Ely Place is still private church property just to the north of Holborn Circus. Nearby are Saffron Hill, Lily Place, Saffron Street, and Herbal Hill, streets which derived their names from the crops of saffron and other herbs the land bore. The bishops produced a health-giving cordial from their herbal gardens, which, with vineyards, were situated on the banks of the river Fleet, which was confined to tunnels by early Victorian development, just west of the present day Farringdon Road. The immediate area has since suffered mixed fortunes. By the middle of the 19th century it had fallen into utter degradation, its notoriety forever recalled by Dickens in *Oliver Twist*; it was not by accident that Fagin's lair is situated on Saffron Hill. The area was badly damaged during the Blitz of World War II. By contrast, it is again rich with gold, not herbal in this case but real bullion and jewels from the precious metal market of neighboring Hatton Garden.

The following list of prices for a pound of saffron was published in the *History of Audley End* by Lord Braybrooke in 1836.

1548	£0.12s.0d	1653	£1.17s.0d
1556	£1. 5s.0d	1664	£3.10s.0d
1614	£3. 3s.4d	1689	£3. 0s.0d
1631	£0.18s.0d	1717	£1. 6s.6d
1647	£1. 2s.0d		

Cultivation of saffron ceased in the British Isles for nearly two hundred years until 1985, when Caroline Riden began to produce small quantities commercially in Wales.

A BUYER'S GUIDE

WORLD PRODUCTION

Spain is the leading producer and exporter of saffron and accounts for around 70% of the world's market. Exports of saffron were worth 2173 million pesetas in 1994[1], the British market being worth 88 million pesetas. Up to 40 metric tons are produced annually in Spain. Over 90% of the staggering crop of 6400,000,000 crocus flowers is of Mancha origin. The main export markets for Mancha saffron are France, Germany, Belgium, Holland, Luxembourg, Denmark, Switzerland, Italy, Sweden, and Britain in Europe. In the rest of the world: North Yemen, Oman, Arab Emirates, Saudi Arabia, Kenya, Singapore, Taiwan, South Korea, Hong Kong, Japan, Malaysia, Canada, Argentina, New Zealand, Australia and the United States of America.

Iran has an estimated production of around 30 metric tons of saffron each year. It is cultivated in two regions: in the southwest, Korassan, and in the north, Kashmar.

Up to 20 metric tons of saffron are harvested in Kashmir's "happy valley"; it is also cultivated in the Uttar Pradesh region of India. The Indian saffron industry is protected by an import ban, therefore most of the production is for the home market, and I have not been able to purchase either in Britain. I did, however, find some high-quality Kashmiri saffron filaments and powdered saffron in the covered market in Freemantle, in western Australia. The "Sun Brand" is packed by the K K Mart company of Srinagar. Each box has the following warranty: "Our company assures to a buyer that this pack contains absolute 100% pure saffron and is free from any alcoholic matter. The buyer may claim full amount of the purchase price if he proves the quality of saffron impure or defective."

I am grateful to Mr. and Mrs. Mahalingan of New Dehli for sending me further samples of "Sun Brand" saffron with which I have prepared many fine meals.

[1] Source I.C.E.X. Madrid

I have found only one English importer of Kashmiri saffron, Mr. Graham Pike of Green Cuisine, who informed me that supplies were becoming erratic and more expensive because of the unfortunate civil strife that has unsettled the state of Kashmir in recent years. In an Indian emporium in Auckland, New Zealand, I found a tiny tin of Lion Brand saffron packed by the Bombay Keshar Company. Unfortunately it was very old and had deteriorated. The shopkeeper informed me he had it in stock for over 10 years; it seems there is not a large demand for saffron in New Zealand yet.

The Abruzzi is the principle region of Italy for saffron production. What does not get consumed in Milan is exported in powdered form. I was surprised to be able to obtain Sardinian saffron in London, both filaments and powder. Also a curious product, powdered saffron suspended in Sardinian extra virgin olive oil; all from Carluccio's in WC2. Italy also imports saffron from Spain and Greece.

Until 1996, I had been unable to find any Greek saffron on retail sale in Britain. Although I was aware of a bulk importer, Mr. Alan Gregory of the Perfection Food Company, his market place is food manufacturers and the bakers of Cornwall. However, in the early spring of 1996 I was visiting a friend's restaurant, Livebait, when the chef Theo called to me from the kitchen, "John, I have some Greek saffron." He showed me a 1 gram plastic box which was branded Krokos Kozanis, Greek Red Saffron Stigmata. It was packed in the "Coupe" style, that is the red filaments only, and appeared to be of high quality and had a deep and pungent aroma.

I then contacted the importer, Alice Seferiades of Odysea Ltd., who informed me that she had just introduced the product into Britain. Alice kindly sent me a lot of information, including the ISO certificate which confirmed that Krokos Kozanis met the strict quality standard of Category 1A. It is grown by the two thousand members of the Cooperative of Saffron, based in the town of Krokos, in the province of Kozanis in western Macedonia, in northern Greece. Between 6 and 12 metric tons are harvested each year and unusually, the fresh, wet stigmas are dried on silk-lined trays, at room temperature. Krokos saffron is exported to all EEC countries, including Sweden and France, where it is used in the production of the liqueur, Benedictine. It is also sold to Hungary, Switzerland, and Japan and will soon become more widely available in Britain.

The French industry has reactivated itself in recent years. There is now very limited production in the Gâtinais, Aquitaine, and Vaucluse. A little French-grown saffron is exported by the Fouchon Company.

The village of Mund in the Haut Valais in Switzerland is nowadays a very minor region, producing just a few kilos each year. It was once a major producing area and it is said that a soldier returning from the wars in Spain hid a few corms in his wig and established the industry during the 17th century. There is also very small production in Austria.

Frances Bissell of the *London Times* told me of some good saffron she found in Morocco, grown in the Atlas mountains. Small crops are also cultivated in Israel, Lebanon, and Turkey.

Commercial production of saffron in Britain is in the hands of one dedicated person. Caroline Riden started growing saffron in the 1980s on her farm in

Wales. Caroline has had to overcome many problems, but now in a good year she produces up to 1 kilo. I discovered her Caer Estyn Farm saffron on sale in Fortnum and Masons in Piccadilly, London. Saffron is a commodity that is subject to re-export. Both Holland and Germany export to Britain, but neither is a producer nation.

A little saffron is also grown by amateur gardeners in England and America (see pages 35–37 for details).

SAFFRON FILAMENTS

Saffron is generally available in two forms, filaments or powder.

Wherever possible, I prefer to see whole saffron filaments in the final presentation of a dish, because they are a sign it has been made with the real thing. For this reason, I recommend purchasing the filaments, as you have the option of using them as they are or grinding them into powder yourself (see page 40).

The British preference is for saffron filaments and they account for little over 80% of total imports, against a maximum of 20% for powder. In Sweden and Italy the reverse is true, their preference being for powdered saffron.

Most professional chefs and food writers prefer to use and write about filaments, as they share a lingering but now unjustified suspicion of most commercial powdered saffron. They may describe filaments as threads, chives, strands, silks, fronds, stems, pistils, blades, or stigmas. Sometimes the filaments are incorrectly identified as stamen, or even golden or yellow stigmas (they are in fact red).

Where do you buy good saffron filaments? If you make only one or two saffron dishes a year, buy it from the supermarket or delicatessen. You will find it in the spice rack or section, in glass jars usually containing 0.4 grams. Look for "Mancha, product of Spain" on the label. If you live in Devon or Cornwall try your local independent chemist or pharmacy. Many still stock saffron, a tradition inherited from the apothecaries of the Middle Ages. Even Boots, the UK national chemist chain, sold saffron in their food section up to the early 1980s. Real saffron filaments can be obtained in drug stores or their equivalent in a number of foreign countries. Such is the international comprehension of the word "saffron," you will probably be understood when purchasing it abroad. I have also found saffron filaments in herbalists and some health food shops.

If you use saffron filaments more readily, buy them directly from a spice merchant/wholesaler or an importer. You will need to purchase a much larger quantity, but the price per gram differential will be very advantageous, up to half that of the retailer. Look in local directories or in the classified advertisements of food magazines, or see Appendix IV of this book. Buy a small amount at first to check the quality. If you are satisfied, return for larger quantities at even lower prices per gram. Much of the cost of saffron in small retail packs is due to the specialized labor needed to weigh and pack it, plus the container itself, glass jars being the most expensive of all.

In checking the quality, what precisely should you be looking for? The packaging should give you some information; brand name and/or packer, region of production, country of origin, a packing or expiration date, the crop year, the moisture content, the weight and a possible quality rating. I have not found nor would I recommend buying saffron loose.

The majority of saffron on sale in Britain and the rest of the world is from Spain. Nearly all of this Spanish saffron is from La Mancha. It is labeled Mancha Selecto, Mancha Superior, and Calidad (Quality) Mancha. More recently the very best Mancha saffron is additionally described as Category 1A, the quality standard of the ISO.

Elizabeth David described Valencia saffron in her book, *Spices, Salt and Aromatics in the English Kitchen*, published in 1970. It is a term I was unfamiliar with, until I purchased a little pack in a chemist shop in Wadebridge, Cornwall. The importer has since informed me that the saffron is in fact grown in La Mancha. It uses the term Valencia, not as a reference to paella, but to the bulk export trade in saffron that passed through the port of Valencia for many hundreds of years. Much of it was bound for the Orient, one of the very few spices to travel east to its markets.

If the Mancha filaments are visible what should you expect to see? Look for a dense bunch of whole filaments intertwined with whitish styles; there should be little or no dust in the box. The filaments should be obviously red, trumpet-shaped, serrated or indented at the distal end. The filaments will be between 20mm and 40mm in length in individual pieces or joined by the style in twos or a full set of three. A small percentage of white, yellow, or orange styles will also be present. They are not waste or padding material, the styles contribute by extending the flavor and aroma range of saffron, but have little crocin to color. Pull 12 styles from a bunch of Mancha saffron and pour a little hot water over them. You will catch the aroma immediately and after a few minutes a flavor will have developed too. Iran also produces a Mancha style saffron called *Kayam*, which means "whole flower." It consists of complete sets of three filaments attached to a long white style. I have a two-gram bundle of *kayam* saffron, tied in the middle like a miniature flaming haystack, a product of very nimble fingers.

There is another international packing standard for saffron, which the Spanish call *coupe*, meaning cut. It consists of the red filaments only, is selected by hand and packed without any white styles. Consequently, it is more expensive than Mancha. More often the exported saffron filaments from Kashmir, Greece, and Iran are packed in this style. In Iran it is called Sargol, meaning "first cut." I prefer Mancha for culinary use as a spice. If however you require maximum coloring power, coupe is potentially the stronger, but more costly and with a slight flavor and aroma loss.

Finally, there are the second grades of Spanish saffron: one is labeled as B, a self-explanatory classification. The other two, known as Rio and Sierra, are often of poor quality, and little is imported into Britain. They are mostly cultivated in Aragon in northeastern Spain. Both have more of a tan or brownish color than red, and a scruffy appearance. The filaments are shorter and the styles are much longer. Sometimes they are harvested from wild crocus, not *Crocus sativus*, and therefore they are not true saffron.

Crop year indicates the harvest date; try to buy the most recent year available. Most European-packed saffron filaments will have an expiration date rather than a packing date. When the saffon leaves the exporter it has 3 to 5 years before its expiration date. If saffron filaments are stored in a light-proof, dry tin or box, away from any source of moisture, they remain in good condition for many years—10 or more is not uncommon. Eventually saffron filaments will become stale, their color will darken then turn to brown and the aroma will decrease, possibly becoming sour. Never store dry saffron filaments in the refrigerator or freezer.

Moisture content is expressed as a maximum permitted percentage, which should not exceed 14%. It is the measurement of the moisture left after the original curing process. You want this figure to be low because water increases the weight, but not the potency or value. Saffron filaments should never be damp or wet when you buy them, but dry and brittle. Incidentally, the milling of saffron filaments into saffron powder dissipates the moisture from the filaments. For this reason, saffron powder is more expensive per gram than filaments because it is more concentrated.

Be careful when buying saffron filaments abroad, as much of it will be *carthamus,* or safflower. If you think about it, it is unlikely that a market trader would display real saffron in the open air; he would lose his stock to the wind, even more so with powder. However, it is possible to buy good saffron at a good price in Spain, but not at the airports where it is expensive. In the last year I have purchased imported saffron filaments from Spain, Sardinia, France, and Iran and domestically cultivated saffron from Wales. I have paid between £2.50 and £6.00 per gram.

POWDERED SAFFRON

I have grown to appreciate the convenience of commercially powdered saffron. Its instant accessibility as an ingredient has overcome any reluctance I may have had. In fact, powdered saffron used straight from the package has come to the rescue on more than one occasion, when I had not prepared an adequate infusion of filaments for a particular recipe. I have noticed, however, that in general terms powdered saffrons have less aroma than saffron filaments.

Retail packs of powdered saffron are usually purchased at the delicatessen, in little, brightly colored packages, sealed and uninspectable, either of 0.100 grs or 0.125 grs, (0.0044 oz), costing 30 to 50 pence each. Each package contains between 40 and 60 ground filaments, which are milled in modern vacuum-controlled machines. Powdered saffron is then packed immediately in light-proof material as it is particularly sensitive to light spoilage. The majority of powdered saffron on sale in Britain is of Italian origin and may be labeled Zafferano. Spain is taking a larger share of the market, now that Category 1A is available in powdered form. I have also found powdered saffron from Sardinia and France. A packet will provide enough saffron to color and flavor 225g (8oz) of long- grain rice, a large loaf of bread, or a succulent fish soup for six.

Look for an expiration date or packing date, some have crop year; yet others have no information other than the weight and the packer. Try holding the package up to the light. Inside you will see a tightly folded paper envelope. Check to be sure the saffron moves freely in the pack; if it moves in one lump, it has been exposed to moisture and will be less potent, but not useless. For security reasons, saffron packages are often stored behind the counter or case, not on the shelf, so you may need to ask the shopkeeper for it. Inspect where it is stored— hopefully in a dry, light-proof tin.

My general recommendation is to buy saffron in filament form and then to powder it yourself (see page 40). Thereby you avoid any remote possibilty of buying adulterated powder, where if there was any impurity it would be easier to conceal. When you open the envelope (be careful as it is easy to spill) you will find what looks like brick dust, a very fine powder, with a slightly burnt hue of red or orange, possibly with tiny flecks of white, the powdered remains of the style, more often found in Spanish powdered saffron than Italian. There should be a delicate aroma.

Sprinkle a tiny amount of the powder into a glass with a teaspoon of cold water. True saffron powder will instantly release a slightly golden, transparent yellow color; followed a few seconds later by its distinctive aroma. At first the water will appear speckled with tiny red dots, then the red color will fade to yellow after a short time.

Some adulterations will color yellow but lack aroma and flavor. Colorant powders, or products labelled Imitation Saffron or Saffron Color, whose packaging mimics true saffron, will contain tartrazine or another chemical dye and are not the real thing. Other false saffrons have been known to color red or even blue. However, I have not found one adulterated pack in the 30 purchases of powdered saffron I have made in Britain during the last year. Some are more potent than others. Remember that real powdered saffron is a red-orange color, never yellow.

FALSE AND NONSAFFRON

You are enjoying a Mediterranean holiday and, while browsing in a local market, you come across a spice stall. There is a huge pile of yellow powder marked as "azafran."The stall holder confirms it is saffron, but it is most likely turmeric.

Turmeric (*curcuma longa*) is an oriental spice, ground from a root similar to ginger. Marco Polo encountered it in 1280, describing it as, "a fruit that resembles saffron, though it is nothing of the kind."Turmeric was substituted for real saffron and was traded widely in Europe by theVenetian spice merchants. It was also used to adulterate saffron and as a cheaper source of yellow dye. The English herbalist Gerrade knew of turmeric by the names of either eastern or Indian saffron. When turmeric is freshly ground it has a peppery aroma with a slightly sour, dusty taste. It is a flavor of the Orient rather than the Mediterranean. Therefore turmeric should not be thought of as a substitute for real saffron; it may color yellow, yet it is not water soluble as saffron is. It has a very different flavor with little aroma when cooked. Turmeric is an indispensable ingredient in the formulation of curry powders, and up to 100,000 acres are cultivated annually in India. It is also used by food processors worldwide to color pre-packaged meals, mustards, pickles and even ice cream. A natural orange-yellow dye is extracted from turmeric, called *curcumin*, E100 on food labels.

A good friend returned from his holiday in Kenya with a pack of turmeric. He knew it would amuse me as its expiration date was the 35th of November 1996! It consists of a polythene bag filled with yellow powder, entitled "saffron" and "zafferano," yet the ingredients state it contains 100% *curcuma longa* or turmeric.

In the same market, even on the same stall you may see something else labeled with a name like saffron. This, at first glance, looks more like real filaments. The stall holder will be most insistent, yet offer you a special deal for a large purchase. This should be a warning to you. A closer examination reveals a small budlike flower, with a central red stem and four or five orange and yellow strands about 1cm in length. It is the dried thistlelike flower heads of *carthamus tinctorius*, more commonly known as safflower. Old English names are bastard saffron, fake or false saffron, dyer's thistle, gold tuft, and saffron thistle. Other names for safflower are American, Mexican, and Egyptian saffron. It is an ancient dye plant able to color both yellow and red, after processing. It really has no use in the kitchen, lacking flavor and aroma, and with only a moderate amount of yellow dye.

I have knowingly purchased "bastard saffron" from a street seller in Prague. I have also been offered it once in London when I asked for saffron. The shopkeeper did not know the difference. Sad to say, several friends have returned from vacations and informed me they have purchased some "cheap saffron." This is an oxymoron.

Other nonsaffrons are made from shredded marigold petals and corn stigmas. They both look a little like Virginia tobacco. Neither is deep red as real saffron is, but are brown or tan colored, nor do they have the trumpet–shaped stigmas of the real thing. Cape saffron is made from the dried flowers of the South African plant, *Lyperia Crocea*; two other Cape plants have also been used to adulterate real saffron, *Crocosma aurea* and *Fritonea aurea*.

In the former Soviet Republic of Georgia, *Izmeretinsky shafran* or Imeretian saffron is found. It is made from dried powdered marigold petals and the savory herb (*satureia hortensis*). This shafran adds the tang distinctive to the region's food, but it is not saffron.

Be wary of buying saffron loose. When exposed to air and light, it loses potency. The moisture content will be higher and it may be adulterated. You could buy a small amount to check the quality; if good, you can return for more.

Finally, there are the chemical food dyes, which are marketed as "saffron color," "imitation saffron" and "paella powder." The powders are usually a vivid orange color, and will contain either E102 Tartrazine, E104 Quinoline Yellow, E107 Yellow ZG, or E110 Sunset Yellow—all are synthetic coal tar dyes, believed to be injurious to health. Many enlightened food manufacturers have now replaced their use with natural products.

Purity Tests

i. Saffron filaments will impart a yellow color to water, alcohol, methanol, ether and chloroform but not to xylene and bezone.

ii. In sulphuric acid, saffron filaments will dye and then turn blue, which changes to red-purple.

iii. No oily stain should be left when filaments are pressed between sheets of uncoated paper, indicating the absence of added vegetable or mineral oil.

iv. Saffron yields about 5 to 7 percent ash. An excess of ash indicates added inorganic matter, which may be artifically colored.

Adulteration of real saffron is nowadays a very rare occurrence. During the Middle Ages, however, it was common. The purity of real saffron was of such immense importance that draconian laws were implemented to act as a merciless deterrent to would-be frauds. Culprits would face being burnt at the stake or buried alive, together with their corrupt merchandise, a fate that befell many. Their temptation was of the Midas kind, when the price of saffron, because of scarcity, exceeded that of gold. Their imposters could take many forms, the aim being to increase the bulk or the weight and the coloring power. Bulk has been increased by mixing safflower, shredded marigold petals, or arnica into real saffron. In previous times, slivers of dried beef, grass, or corn silks have been detected. Very rarely you may find that poor quality control has allowed waste floral matter (pollen, stamens, etc.) from *Crocus sativus* to be packed. Weight can be increased by moisture—partial soaking of filaments with alcohol or water was one method. The saffron will mildew or rot in a short time. If the packaging is stained yellow, do not purchase it. Other methods involve coating filaments with wax, oils, fats, and honey.

In the first century A.D., Pliny (A.D. 23–70) the Roman author wrote *Natural History*, much of it devoted to medicinal plants. He recorded how saffron would be moistened, mixed with fat, or otherwise tampered with. Pliny said, "Nothing is so subject to sophistication as true saffron. If a man lay his hand upon it, he shall hear it crack, as if it were brittle and ready to burst; for that which is moist, yields in the hand and has no voice." This is still good advice.

The coloring power of poor-quality or spent saffron has been increased by use of many dye compounds: Iodine, annatto, turmeric, and coal tar, for example. Some of these dye powders have confusing brand names like "safranin." They are unpleasant and should be avoided as they have been linked to hyperactivity in children and are not recommended for aspirin-sensitive people.

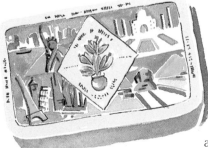

Powdered saffron has offered more opportunities for the fraud. Barium sulphate, nitrate (salt peter) and borax have been used. If borax is used, then nitrate must be too. If not, the borax and saffron powder will not burn—a test carried out by wise merchants. Brick dust and ground rock have also been discovered, as has powdered red sandalwood, powdered pernambucowood, and powdered red capsicum. If the possibility of buying false saffron powder concerns you, again I suggest that you buy whole saffron filaments and powder them yourself (see page 40).

This portrays an overly gloomy picture of the modern saffron industry. It is, however, the chemical food dye companies we need to worry about, by marketing their manufactured dye compounds in packaging that is similar to true saffron and by using brand names that are based on the words "crocus" and "saffron," their aim is to intentionally mislead the consumer, by the substitution of, at best, a neutral substance, at worst, a harmful one, for the benign and nourishing stigmas of *Crocus sativus*.

A reputable packer or importer of saffron has far too much at stake to even contemplate any trickery; you will not encounter any problems with purity, but there will be, however, a variance in potency between brands, and the country of origin.

THE MYTH'S END

Saffron is the most costly spice, but is it expensive? In times of scarcity, its price has exceeded that of gold. This is not the case today as the price of gold is well over that of the price of top-quality Mancha saffron filaments. (Be aware that a shortage of saffron brought about by a bad harvest could change the current pricing dramatically). And as little as ¹⁄₁₀ of a gram can transform the mundane into the splendid.

Saffron provides nutrients, aroma, flavor and it colors with the most alluring hue of the culinary rainbow. Is there any other ingredient that offers so much yet costs so little? Saffron adds value and is valuable, but is it expensive? I'll let you decide.

GROW YOUR OWN

IT MAY BE SURPRISING to learn that you can grow saffron in your own garden. But know that *Crocus sativus* can be remarkably shy of producing flowers, particularly during the first year. However, it was grown successfully by the "crokers" of Essex for nearly 400 years. Moreover, the plant can thrive in diverse conditions, ranging from temperate climates to the more extreme climates of La Mancha and Iran.

Suppliers of saffron corms (bulbs) are listed in Appendix IV. But Caroline Riden, who cultivates saffron commercially in Wales, has advised caution when purchasing *Crocus sativus* corms, even from a reputable seed merchant. Caroline has shown me a packet which depicts a different crocus variety to the true saffron crocus, yet the packet is labeled *Crocus sativus*. Caroline grew these imposter corms and now believes them to be *Crocus cartwrightianus*, a related variety, possibly one of the true saffron crocus parents, but not the real thing. *Crocus orsinii* is another possible parent of *Crocus sativus* and is a native of Ascoli in Italy.

First you must choose your site. The ideal sites are south facing and shade free. The soil needs to be a light loam that is well drained, to prevent the corms from rotting. The soil must also be nutrient rich. The Spanish farmers dig in manure, but horse or cow dung can be used as can compost and leaf mold; avoid chemical fertilizers. It should be dug in during the spring to a depth of half a meter (20 inches). The site should be kept weed free and it should be hoed and given a light dressing of compost a week before planting the corms. *Crocus sativus* requires all the energy soil and sun can provide to generate the flowers containing the prized stigmas.

Modern instructions recommend planting corms at a depth of 6 to 8 cm (3 inches). But the majority of the old husbandry books I have consulted from the 17th and 18th centuries recommend a deeper planting of 12 to 14 cm (5 to 6 inches). My experimental plantings in Devon and Sussex suggest that the deeper planting is best. In extreme conditions, Duncan Ross of Poyntzfield Nursery in north Scotland suggests putting the corms in under glass and in pots rather than in open ground. Duncan harvests a small crop each year, and dries the wet stigmas on his kitchen window sill. I suspect this is the northern limit for saffron production, although it was once cultivated commercially in Zeeland, Holland.

It may prove to be disappointing but often in the first year your corms will produce only the green, chivelike leaves. Be patient, as this is part of the process of the corms maturing and adapting to your conditions. Bear in mind that 14 flowers will only produce $\frac{1}{10}$ of a gram of dried saffron.

You may also find that you will need to protect your corms from the ravenous appetites of rats and rabbits, among other pests and predators.

Last season's corms should be lifted in the spring and replanted in June or July. *Crocus sativus* is sterile, and propagation is achieved by division of the cormlets that form around the main corm. Each season will increase your corm stock. When you lift them, be selective and keep only the best for replanting. As the corms mature they will produce more flowers, up to three on consecutive mornings. Each season you will need to relocate your saffron garden, leaving the previous site fallow for several years (up to 20!) before replanting in the same ground.

In Kashmir during the first year, the corms are planted at a higher density and left to grow for one or two years. After having developed sufficiently, they are then planted in the production area in long mounds of soil to provide better drainage and often amongst almond trees, which crop at the same time of year and produce additional income from the same plot of land and labor. The corms will remain in production for between 12 and 15 years, then the site will be planted with wheat or mustard for three years before the saffron crocuses are returned.

You can expect to harvest from mid-October onwards and the harvest can last until Christmas. Pick the flowers the morning they show, which can be difficult as they are so beautiful; it is back-breaking work. Return to your kitchen and set about removing the delicate long red stigmas from the crocus flowers. Squeeze the style, the white part, between your thumb and forefinger and gently pull.

Tweezers may help. Place the wet stigmas on a sheet of aluminum foil then examine your fingers to see how yellow they have become. Bring the oven up to low heat, maximum 100°C (200°F). Place the foil and stigmas on a baking tray and put them in the oven and close the door. The first step is to "sweat" the stigmas, which will take 2 to 3 minutes. Now open the oven door and leave it open for the rest of the drying period. Give the baking tray a good shake or gently stir the stigmas. Continue to gently cure the stigmas; they are being dried not cooked. Remove the tray from the oven and inspect. The stigmas will have shrunk and will have begun to resemble saffron. Check to be sure the foil is not too hot and that the stigmas are evenly dry; the random wet one will rot and could damage the rest when stored. You may need to return them to the oven for a few more minutes, but continue to be watchful. If you are lucky enough to have a large crop, dry it in batches. Be extra diligent with this process to avoid burning your precious crop. Your reward is the satisfaction of cooking your first meal with your own home-grown saffron.

Landscape gardeners could also make good use of *crocus sativus* to create a sweep of purple at an otherwise barren time of year and also as a cash crop.

The saffron that was cultivated in Essex was considered to be the best in the world, albeit by Englishmen. I wonder if the industry will ever be reestablished, and if England could again become an exporter of the most highly esteemed spice in the world.

HOW TO USE
SAFFRON

"THE PINCH"

What is a "pinch" of saffron filaments? There can be a huge variation. How large are your fingers and what is the size of the box the pinch is being taken from? A pinch from a 1-gram box will be smaller than a professional chef's pinch from a 25 gram tin—one man's pinch is another man's pile.

For both color and flavor, the majority of recipes in this book require approximately ¹⁄₁₀ of a gram of Mancha saffron filaments, too small a quantity to weigh on kitchen scales. Therefore I have counted out the individual filaments in each recipe, 40–50 filaments being the equivalent of ¹⁄₁₀ of a gram. I have counted only the red filaments of Mancha saffron. The white styles are not counted, but are included in the dish. If you are using Iranian "coupe"-style saffron, the red count will be the same.

The accuracy of this count method is not completely precise, as filaments vary in length and thickness, and some are broken. However you really need to establish your own measure of saffron filaments as it is tiresome to count them out on every occasion. With a little practice you will be able to train your eye to gauge your portion with consistency. As a guide, try dividing a 1-gram box into 10 equal portions, a ½-gram box into 5 portions or a 0.4-gram jar into 4 portions; the mass of each portion can then be judged as a basis for your measure, that is approximately ¹⁄₁₀ of a gram. A 1-gram box contains approximately 540 individual saffron filaments, the yield of 180 hand-picked crocus flowers or 10 measures of 50 filaments.

You may prefer to adopt a different formula, which is to count the filaments per person. For example, a yield of two crocus flowers is six filaments — try this amount per person plus a further six filaments for the pot. Your own taste or a recipe may dictate three filaments or nine per person. A little experimentation based on this formula will provide you with a benchmark, a standard measure to work to and from.

Either of these methods is preferable to the vague pinch or generous pinch or the ¼ or ½ teaspoon prescribed by other writers. In one cookbook I found that the author seemed to think that just one filament would be enough for a risotto. I have seen television chefs adding saffron filaments by the boxful, straight into the pot. In a recent magazine article ¼ ounce or 7 grams is recommended for a cake recipe; is this a misprint, or is it an ill-considered reprint of a 16th-century recipe? Elizabeth David's method was rather quaint: she would cover an old, pre-decimal sixpence with filaments and use that as her measure.

Be aware of the variants when portioning your saffron. Are you cooking for two or eight people? If you require only to color a dish then half the measure may suffice. Know the potency of the saffron you are using and allow for the duration of the infusion time.

By way of further experimentation put just one filament into a ramekin with 1 tablespoon of hot water. Allow several hours for it to infuse, overnight is best. You may be surprised by the development just one filament can achieve. Taste and smell the infusion liquid, notice the color; the potency of one filament can be assessed and the basis of your measure decided as a result.

"The cook who is mean with his saffron is capable of seducing his grandmother," wrote Norman Douglas in his book *Venus in the Kitchen*. How true.

THE USE OF SAFFRON FILAMENTS

Saffron filaments differ from other ingredients, as they need to be activated before use. Many cooks are unaware of this. Consequently, saffron's virtues have eluded them. Some are reluctant to ever try saffron again. Others, professional chefs included, have used too many filaments (the generous pinch) and have overwhelmed a dish with unpalatable medicinal flavor. What quantity of saffron filaments and how to use them effectively requires a little forethought and practice.

To activate filaments, either method is available to you:
1. Liquid - Heat - Time .... Infusion
2. Gentle Heat - Grinding .... Powdered

THE INFUSION

The three valuable culinary essences of saffron are water soluble. Soaking filaments will allow them to rehydrate, thereby releasing their properties to the liquid. They will expand, swelling eventually to their original size. This takes time, but differing liquids and the application of heat will allow the saffron to "brew" more rapidly.

The infusion of filaments should be the first step in the cooking process, starting 30 minutes, 1 hour, even a day before the final assembly of the other ingredients. How and when the infusion is used in the cooking process will also have bearing on the flavor, aroma and color of the finished dish.

Placed in hot water, filaments will instantly start to release color and aroma. The flavor develops more slowly, dry and bitter with a honeylike aftertaste, when tried neat. After five minutes you will notice you have more saffron than you started with; the filaments have begun to swell. The color will have intensified and saffron's genial aroma permeated the room.

If you are unfamiliar with this technique and have some saffron filaments in your kitchen, start an infusion now. Count out 40 individual whole filaments, place them in a cup and add 2 tablespoons of boiling hot water. Leave it to infuse, return at 5 minutes, 10 minutes, 30 minutes, 1 hour, 2 hours, overnight, and 24 hours. Look at the infusion to gauge the color, and to smell and taste it. This simple experiment will give you a measure of how potent your saffron is and when optimum development is reached. You could also try dipping strips of kitchen paper towel into the infusion for 1 second at the above intervals. Allow the papers to dry and then compare with each other. You will clearly see how much more coloring power has developed with the passing of time. However, you may notice a slight loss of aroma and flavor by the end of 24 hours. You will never just add a pinch of saffron directly to a recipe ever again.

Aroma is the most delicate of saffron's charms, so care is needed to protect it. Long-term infusions should be covered with a saucer or plastic wrap. Use a light-proof vessel, a cup or a mug, as these will preserve flavor and the nutritional benefits of the filaments. Coloring power will intensify with time, and eventually the filaments will appear to be exhausted (around 12 hours), ghost-like and pale, having been bled of all their goodness and color by the liquid.

POWDERING SAFFRON FILAMENTS

Grinding saffron filaments into powder is a relatively simple and quick process. With a little careful practice you will soon master it. Care needs to be taken during the heating of your precious filaments, as it is all too easy to burn them. With this in mind I have opted for the following method.

I dry my filaments in a pale-colored, dry, heavy saucepan, where it is much easier to keep an eye on them, than grilling or baking in the oven. The idea is to dry them not to cook them. As an added precaution, because of previous disasters I do this off the heat, in a constantly cooling pan.

I start by placing the pan on a medium heat for between 30 seconds and 1 minute, depending on the amount of saffron. I then tip in the filaments and immediately remove the pan from the heat. I shake the pan to dissipate the heat through the filaments, then leave them for 2 minutes to allow them to "cure." If they show any signs of darkening they are too hot and ready to burn, tip them out of the pan and leave to cool. You may be lucky; if burnt, filaments are useless. The heating awakens *safrannal*, saffron's delicate aroma. The lower the temperature the less safrannal will be lost.

I then find I can crumble the cured filaments between my fingers. I prefer however to grind them in a small, polished, brass mortar and pestle. Large mortars tend to lose saffron powder in nicks and scratches and loose-grained or unpolished wooden pestles will absorb it. Five seconds work with the brass pestle and I have a fine powder, but not as fine as commercially milled saffron powder.

You can crush the toasted filaments in the pan with the back of a spoon. Or transfer to a tablespoon then crush with the back of a teaspoon, grinding it from side to side. Do this over a pale surface in case any is spilt. Another method is to wrap the filaments in aluminum foil and crush them with a rolling pin. With Mancha saffron you will find that the red filaments crush down to powder very quickly, the whitish style requires more work.

THE USE OF AN INFUSION

Often, I will find that saffron filaments are the first ingredient I prepare but the last that I add to a dish. Their cooking takes place separately, away from the main pot. The golden rules of using a saffron infusion are: (1) for maximum color add it at the beginning of the cooking process with high heat and (2) for maximum flavor and aroma, add the infusion near the end of the cooking and with a lower heat. I usually do half and half, beginning and end.

An infusion can also be "held" and then used at the very last moment, to impart a final intensification of aroma and flavor in particular, and of course color. This method is used in professional kitchens where an infusion is prepared often in white wine, then held in bain-marie during service. A measure of this infusion will either be mixed into a sauce immediately before serving or used directly on a finished plated dish, often with spectacular results. This technique has a similarity to the way saffron is used in Iran and in India. For an example, refer to the recipe for Persian Rice (see page 95). A small amount of cooked white rice is placed in a bowl with the infusion liquid. The rice absorbs the liquid, the yellowed grains are then scattered over the remaining mound of white rice, creating a golden peak. In Indian recipes, a saffron infusion will be drizzled over a dish immediately before it is served.

A saffron infusion can also be placed on the table and used as a condiment; to spoon into soup or pasta for example. Finally, saffron tea is an extension of the infusion process. Allow 60 filaments to brew in a liter of hot water for 12 hours. Serve the saffron tea concentrate hot or cold with a splash of lemon juice and dollop of honey.

INFUSION LIQUIDS FOR SAFFRON FILAMENTS

Although boiling hot water will give a good early development, as the water cools it becomes less efficient. There are other liquids you can use, that will continue to work more effectively than water. They include: white wine; dry, pale vermouths; gin; vodka; even Cointreau. The alcohol works well because it acts as a solvent on the filaments. Similarly, because of their acidity, cider, rice, and white wine vinegars and the citrus juices of lemon and orange will accelerate the development of the infusion. Two particularly charming liquids that promote a good development and evoke the flavors of the Middle East are orange flower and rose waters.

You will find many recipes that recommend infusing saffron filaments in hot stock or the hot cooking liquid for a few minutes before returning to the pot. This does help, but the development of the infusion is confined, because of the fat content of most stocks. Remember the essences of saffron are water soluble. It would be better to use one of the liquids listed above and then add the infusion to the pot. However, it is possible to infuse saffron filaments successfully in hot milk.

I have experimented with shortcuts in the infusion process. One is to make several individual infusions of 40 filaments in 2 tablespoons of hot water. I let the infusion develop for 2 hours, then I pour each into the individual compartments of an ice cube tray and freeze them. When required, each cube can be used virtually instantly by melting in a saucepan before incorporating into a recipe.

Another method is to heat an infusion in a microwave oven at half power for 1 minute—a curious liaison of ancient and modern.

A further method is to toast or dry-fry the filaments briefly before adding the liquid. Care is needed as saffron filaments burn very easily. I use the same method as for powdering filaments (see page 40). I dry-fry filaments in a heavy, preheated saucepan off the heat. After 2 minutes, I add the liquid and return the pan to the heat to simmer for a few minutes.

Note that saffron filaments will entwine themselves in whisks and enmesh themselves in sieves and strainers. Therefore, always add the filaments to the infusion liquid after using these utensils. Or, use powdered saffron, which will remain in the solution.

LESS IS MORE

We tend to think of saffron only in terms of making spectacular saffron recipes: paella, risotto, cakes— yet this is only part of saffron's repertoire. The ancient carpet weavers of Persia appreciated saffron's yellow; its ability to mix with and enhance other hues was equally as impor- tant to them. A similar philosophy would be well employed in the modern kitchen, as saffron will illuminate the stage for other flavors to dance upon. When the normal pinch of most recipes is reduced to just a few filaments, judi- ciously used, saffron becomes an enhancer of tastes rather than the vanguard flavor.

It is fun to conjure with saffron in this way, and I have enlivened many everyday meals, such as omelettes and stews. I have powdered just 9 Mancha filaments and added it to the flour of a Yorkshire pudding mix. My aim was to have an attractive, more appetizing color. I cooked a stronger flavored pudding, not of saffron but a greater sum of its parts. It was served at a family lunch, and everybody commented on how good the Yorkshire was—"very tasty," "smoky," "meaty," and "more intense" were the reviews. I kept that saffron secret to myself at the time.

I have made deep yellow pancakes with a pronounced saffron flavor. I grind 30 filaments into powder then mix it in with the flour before making the batter. On other occasions I have used much less saffron, which I have infused in hot milk for an hour, then added to the batter to make a softer lemon-colored pan- cake. A little chopped saffron, dry-fried and incorporated into a tempura batter makes for interesting hot spots of color in the pearllike glaze of tempura prawns or vegetables. Your favorite bread recipe can be transformed by a little saffron, powdered into the flour or whole filaments infused in hot water and incor- porated with the yeast into the dough. Dazzle your dinner guests with a bejewelled bread and butter pudding. Cake, biscuit and pastry mixtures can also be enhanced. A liquid saffron concentrate can be painted onto the pastry of sweet and savory pies, the way food was "endored" in medieval times. With an artist's paintbrush many intricate coloring applications can be accomplished, particularly with cake icing and desserts.

My mother, Margaret, was during her lifetime an accomplished cook. She taught me many of the basics of good culinary practice for which I am very grateful. Not only my family, but many others will testify to the high degree of skill she mastered in making meringue pies. During my "Mexican period" we transformed the usual lemon, by using limes, into the exotic and tropical Margarita Meringue Pie, adding both tequilla and Triple-sec to the tangy and potent, green-colored filling. My father, John, would then deliver the pies to Cafe Pacifico, the racous London Cantina. I have since made gilded meringue with powdered saffron, combining it with the sugar before beating with the egg whites, for an even yellow coloration and saffron flavor. I have also used whole filaments, dry-fried, for a more brazen effect. On one occasion I used a few drops of a saffron infusion to increase the color of the lemon filling with a minimum effect to the citrus flavor.

Dairy products offer a host of opportunities for the epicure of saffron. Cheese and butter both have saffron added to them during manufacture, for obvious reasons. You can work powdered saffron into hard butter or margarine, before adding it to a cake recipe; also you could put saffron butter on a tea time table or serve it with baked potatoes.

Eggs have been enjoyed with saffron's influence for centuries. Either a tiny pinch of powder or a few filaments (6) infused in a tiny amount of hot milk will produce both radiant omelettes and scrambled eggs, to accompany smoked salmon. Likewise the egg mixture of flans and quiche can be enriched. A truly golden soufflé will embellish every cook's reputation, savory as a starter or drizzled with a light honey for dessert. Both the egg sauces, mayonnaise and hollandaise take on more color and character (For more about this, see recipes on pages 75–76.) Why make a white sauce when it is so easy to make a yellow one? Powdered saffron can be mixed with flour in any roux-based sauce preparation.

I like to watch the pleasure on friends' faces when they crack the crust of a crème bruleé to discover a primose-colored cream, veined with long crimson filaments. Crema Catalana benefits similarly. Custard is another willing victim of saffron's seduction. Sherry trifle crowned in this way is a sumptuous treat. An instant garnish for soups or desserts is made by stirring a little powdered saffron into cream. Try to let the flavor develop for a while, then stir again before serving.

Indian cooks add a few filaments, infused in the minimum of liquid, to yogurt, then let it bleed, before serving as a rippled table condiment, and also as a festive treatment for Lassi, the yogurt long drink. A little saffron will underscore most Indian curry recipes, acting as an aristocratic catalyst to the other spices.

A multitude of grains can be colored or flavored or both. Rice, of course, is a perfect host, but rice pudding with saffron is much less common, as is couscous. Amber-toned cannellini beans in a salad of white endive and rich, dark plum tomatoes, sliced lengthwise, dressed with olive oil, are an eye-catching combination. "Zafferano" pasta and noodles have an easy co-existence. For example, make a paste with saffron powder and a little hot water (like making mustard), stir into pasta after you have drained it. If you make your own pasta you could try blending powdered saffron into the flour, or an infusion can be added with the water as you make the dough. The béchamel sauce of lasagne could also be pleasantly yellowed, as could its partner across the Ionian Sea, moussaka. A Scottish friend suggested saffron porridge. I am not so enthusiastic for saffron at breakfast time, other than in bread.

Saffron's relationship with meat is less humorous. To my taste, pork can have difficulties with saffron. Chicken, however, triumphs. Rabbit is also good. In Morocco, saffron is added to tagine of lamb and in the Emmental region of Switzerland, Ammitaler Schoffigs is prepare: a rich stew of lamb and saffron, which is also sometimes an ingredient of Rosti. A few filaments crumbled into a long-cooking oxtail stew (and soup) has been a good discovery. As has a little saffron added to other aromatics and herbs in slow-cooked beef casserole, like goulash (unified with paprika) or even chili con carne. It may seem wasteful to use saffron in brown stew, but the cooking liquid in both recipes has a beautiful burnished, and polished effect, as will saffron–enriched gravy. Stuffing for roasts present more chances for subtle experimentation and sunny saffron dumplings will cheer any winter's broth.

I found in La Mancha that a hint of *azafran* brings out the seasonal flavor of partridge; other game birds, such as pheasant or grouse could also feel the gentle touch of saffron's wand. Tripe is treated delicately with *safran* in several French recipes. The bright and glossy rouille of the Mediterranean coast depends on *safran* for its warm orange color. In Argentina, *azafran* is an ingredient of a marinade for meat, prior to grilling.

I encourage you to improvise with the ethereal characteristics of saffron. It will tease your taste buds, while adding backbone and posture to a recipe. The wealth of a dish will be increased, as will its elegance. The requisite trace that will embellish the commonplace is for you to decide. The saffron trinity of flavor, aroma, and color allows for many experiments and ensures a bright future for this regal and most ancient spice.

SERVE IT FORTH

Saffron's use in the kitchens of England from the Roman period to the eve of the French revolution

The decline of the Roman Empire led to the collapse of its trading and distribution networks in western and northern Europe, thereby creating a great scarcity of spices from the East, Persia, India, and China.

The westward expansion of the Arabs brought a degree of stability to the Mediterranean and the reintroduction of many spices. European merchants were able to trade in Constantinople and Alexandria, the warehouse cities at the western end of the Silk Road that stretched eastwards to China and to the Spice Islands of Ceylon and the Moluccas.

The whole of the north coast of Africa fell under Arab control and from there they invaded first Spain in 711A.D. and then Sicily in 827A.D., where the cooks of the victorious army created what was to become the island's national dish: *Pasta con le Sarde,* which is made of sardines and pasta, baked in the layered *beryān* style of Persia. The sauce is made from mashed sardines, fennel, pine nuts, currants, and a generous pinch of *za'farān*. The Normans were the next to conquer Sicily and Southern Italy, where they displayed Byzantine rule before their invasion of England in 1066. They reintroduced a range of foodstuffs forgotten by the English since the Roman period 500 years earlier.

The color of food and its final presentation was of great importance in the kitchens of the Middle Ages. Yellow sauces made with saffron would be marbled or striped red with powdered sandalwood. Green came from parsley or spinach juice, and blue from indigo. Some sauces were made only for lavish presentation at grand banquets, while others were to be eaten.

Many foods, especially roasted meat, were endored, that is, painted with a saffron wash, which then would be baked, giving an opulent gilded appearance to a dish. In France, *saffranum* was used to make *jaunette*, a yellow sauce for eggs and was mixed with egg yolks to gild spit-roasted meats.

One staple food of the period was frumenty, a thick pudding or pottage or porridge of wheat or barley grains that is cooked in cow's or almond milk with egg yolks and warmly colored with saffron. In the great houses of the nobility, frumenty was a popular accompaniment to roasted venison.

The Forme of Cury was compiled by the master cooks of Richard II, and was published in 1378. Over half the recipes call for "safron," as a colorant, or as a spice for flavor and aroma. Many of the recipes are the ancestors of food we still enjoy today. The saffron recipes include a three-colored soup, a saffron soup, an egg and cheese tart, an onion tart, marinade for fish, a mussel broth and a fish jelly, braised chicken in a sauce of pine nuts and saffron, Tartes of Flesh (small birds in a pie), a chicken and almond *blancmange*, pigeon casserole with herbs and spices, and a mixed fruit and vegetable chutney.

Two of the many dishes served at the coronation banquet of Henry IV on the 13th of October, 1399 were *Doucetye*, a honey and *saffroun* quiche, and *Crustard Lumbard*, a custard flan with cream, dates, prunes, and *saffroun*.

Various books and manuscripts from the 15th century give further insights into the cuisine of the late Middle Ages. By this time much of the *saffroun* used by cooks in England would have been cultivated in Essex, at the then named Chypping Walden. For example: *Tench in cyueye*, which is a fish soup of tench, flavored with ale and *safroun*; a tart, then known as a *cofyn*, with pastry colored by *safroun*, filled with egg and beef or veal bone marrow; *pertrych stewyde*, partridge stewed with cloves, mace, ginger, and saffron; *conyngys in graveye*, a rabbit cooked in a sauce of *safroun*, ginger, galingale, cinnamon, cloves, and sugar; a *llowes de Mutton*, which are lamb steaks basted with *safroun*; stewed mutton; a savory meat custard; and a casserole of pork.

From a manuscript in the collection of Samuel Pepys, which was probably written by Dame Juliana Berners around 1486, there are recipes for roasted lampreys with ale, pepper, and *faffroun*; eggs in a broth of milk, with cheese, ginger, pepper, and *faffroun*; and skinned chickens, stuffed with a mixture of pork, egg yolks, currants, herbs, salt, and *faffroun*. The stuffed birds were then inserted back into the skin, which was smoothed down, then the birds were parboiled and roasted. From the same manuscript is the Rice of Genoa, an interesting and delicious recipe with more than a passing similarity to modern-day risotto, as the rice is cooked in beef stock with added bone marrow, *faffroun* and salt. Finally the rice was moistened with almond milk.

There is a 1381 reference to *Tartys in Apples*, an early version of apple pie. The instructions call for using apples, pears, figs, and raisins, are "color with safron well and do it in a coffin, do it forth to bake well," spiced with ginger, nutmeg, cinnamon, and saffron. Other desserts consisted of spiced pears, quinces, and custards, all mellowed with a yellow glow. Fruit fritters, sweet rice pudding, and even the currently fashionable bread and butter pudding are prepared with saffron in 15th-century manuscripts. Saffron bread was also eaten at the beginning of Lent.

In the 16th century, Andrew Boorde published a recipe for a meatball soup, cooked in beef stock and almond milk with saffron and cloves. In the *Good Huswife's Handmaid* of 1594 there is a recipe for Poached Forcemeat Dumplings. Forcemeat is like Christmas mincemeat and is made from eggs, currants and bread crumbs flavored with ginger, cinnamon, and saffron. It is at this time that Shakespeare colored "warden (pear) pies" with saffron in *A Winter's Tale*.

In Robert May's *The Accomplisht Cook*, published in 1660, there is a good recipe for split peas in a rich saffron butter sauce, and an oatmeal stuffing for birds with mace, dates, and saffron. Also published in 1660 was Fervase Markham's, *A Way to Health*, with a recipe for a Spice Cake that calls for "a good deal of saffron in the milk," and is combined with other aromatics, cloves, mace, and rose water.

There is an interesting recipe for a Cuscasooee of Capons in Charles Carter's, *The Compleat City and Country Cook* (1732): a chicken is stuffed and boiled, rice is added to the cooking juices then simmered. When ready, a small amount of rice is removed and mixed in a bowl with the saffron infusion. It is then returned to the main body of white rice as a golden garnish, very much in the Persian style. In 1783, John Farley published the *London Art of Cookery*. In it is found a Postage of Vermajelly with Capon, which is a rich chicken soup served with saffron-colored vermicelli.

The late 17th and early 18th centuries saw the beginning of the decline in saffron's popularity in the English kitchen. In part it was replaced by flavors from the New World, vanilla and cacao. Production of English saffron in Essex began to falter as food fashion changed, other cheaper sources of yellow dye were found and imports of Spanish saffron undercut the English growers.

Here is a mosaic of recipes that depicts saffron's place in the history of the table, of food, and of eating in Western Europe for over twelve centuries.

ALITER IUS IN AVIBUS SAFFRON
NUT SAUCE FOR ROASTED POULTRY AND FOWL

50 saffron filaments, powdered,
   or 1 packet powdered saffron
½ teaspoon black pepper, ground
1 teaspoon chopped fresh parsley
1 teaspoon celery seed or lovage
½ teaspoon chopped mint leaves
2 ounces hazelnuts, toasted and
   chopped

½ cup white wine
1 tablespoon honey
1 tablespoon white wine vinegar
1 cup chicken stock
1 teaspoon extra virgin olive oil
1 sprig of mint
1 celery stalk, finely chopped

In a mortar, grind together the saffron, pepper, parsley, celery seed, and mint. Add the nuts to the mortar and continue to grind together. Transfer to a small mixing bowl. Add the wine, honey, vinegar, and stock and mix well.

Heat the olive oil in a saucepan and add the sauce. Bring to a boil, then simmer for 25 minutes to reduce.

Pour the sauce over a bird prepared for roasting and work it into the cuts and crevices. Return the bird to the hot oven and finish cooking 5 to 10 minutes. Garnish with fresh mint and chopped celery.

The Roman Recipes of Apicius

IUS IN ANGUILLA
SAFFRON, PLUM, AND WINE SAUCE FOR POACHED EELS

50 saffron filaments, powdered,
   or 1 packet powdered saffron
½ teaspoon ground black pepper
1 teaspoon celery seed or lovage
½ teaspoon savory
1 teaspoon finely chopped onion
3 plums or damsons, peeled and
   finely sliced

6 tablespoons white wine
2 teaspoons white wine vinegar
1 cup fish stock
1 tablespoon extra virgin olive oil
2 pounds poached eels or other
   poached fish
Fresh mint leaves for garnish

In a mortar, grind together the saffron, pepper, celery seed, and savory. Mix in the onion, then the plums. Mash them together.

In a saucepan heat the wine, vinegar, and fish stock. When simmering add the sauce from the mortar and stir. Continue to simmer for 20 minutes to reduce. Stir in the olive oil. Spread the sauce on a deep plate and place the poached fish on it. Pour a little sauce over the fish and garnish with the mint leaves.

The Roman Recipes of Apicius

TART IN EMBER DAY
ONION TART

1 ⅓ cups heavy cream
30 saffron filaments, powdered, or
    ½ packet powdered saffron
12 ounces premade pastry crust
2 large onions, sliced
1 tablespoon butter
3 eggs plus 2 extra egg yolks
⅓ cup raisins, plumped in hot water

⅓ cup currants
¼ teaspoon ground ginger
¼ teaspoon ground cinnamon
¼ teaspoon ground nutmeg
2 ½ tablespoons sugar
½ teaspoon salt
1.25ml (¼ tsp) black pepper, ground

Warm the cream and add the saffron (do not boil). Remove from the heat and allow saffron to infuse.

Roll out the pastry. Line a 9-inch flat pie plate with the pastry. Crimp the edges and bake for 10 minutes at 400°. Remove and allow to cool.

Sauté the onions in the butter until golden. Drain and reserve.

Beat the eggs and the extra yolks together, then add the warm cream–saffron mixture. Continue to beat the two together. Stir in the onions, raisins, currants, spices, and salt.

Pour the mixture into the pie shell and bake at 350° for 25 to 30 minutes or until set.

The Forme of Cury, 1378

A MEDIEVAL 'ENDORING' FLUID FOR ROAST MEATS

"The gilding of the roast," from a 15th-century manuscript.

50 saffron filaments, powdered,
  or 1 packet powdered saffron
3 tablespoons white wine vinegar

2 tablespoons unsalted butter
2 ½ tablespoons sugar
1 egg yolk, lightly beaten

Combine half of the saffron with the wine vinegar and set aside to infuse.
Very gently, melt the butter in a saucepan, then add the remaining saffron and cook very slowly until the butter takes on a good yellow color.
Start to add the sugar, a little at a time, and stir to incorporate into the butter.
Then add the vinegar–saffron infusion and cook on a low heat until syrupy.
Remove from the heat and allow to cool slightly, then stir in the egg yolk.
Return to a low heat and cook until the mixture thickens.
Brush over meat for the last 5 minutes of roasting time. Do not allow to burn.

SALSA COMUN

Spice mixtures, such as the next two recipes, were formulated to standardize the spicing of many different recipes (savory or sweet) and even drinks like mulled wine. I find them useful for Indian recipes and for brushing on roasted meats to form a spiced crust. This spice mixture comes from Ruperto de Nola, the 16th-century cook to the King of Naples. It is savory and does not contain sugar.

3 parts ground cinnamon
2 parts ground cloves
1 part ground ginger

1 part ground pepper
½ part ground coriander
½ part powdered saffron

Grind the spices together in a mortar then store in an airtight, light-proof jar.

SCAPPI'S SPICE MIXTURE

Bartolomeo Scappi was the cook to Pope Pius V. This spice mix is from his *Opera dell'Arte del Cucinare*, an early and influential Italian cookbook. It was republished in Jill Norman's book, *The Complete Book of Spices*.

24 cinnamon sticks
¼ ounce saffron filaments dry-fried
   and powdered
2 ½ tablespoons whole cloves
1 generous tablespoon ground ginger

1 generous tablespoon grated nutmeg
½ tablespoon grains of paradise
   or 1 green cardamom pod
1 tablespoon packed brown sugar

Crush the cinnamon sticks, then grind all the other spices together. Store in an airtight, light-proof jar.

MEDIEVAL SPICED BREAD AND BUTTER PUDDING

This is from a 15th-century manuscript.

Serves 4 to 6

40 saffron filaments, powdered
   or 1 packet powdered saffron
10 ½-inch thick slices good
   white bread
½ cup unsalted butter
1 ⅓ cups white wine
4 eggs

¼ teaspoon salt
¼ cup sugar
2 ½ cups almond milk (see page 53)
¼ teaspoon ground ginger
¼ teaspoon ground cinnamon
¼ teaspoon ground cloves
¼ teaspoon ground mace

Slowly toast the bread until golden, then generously butter and cut the crusts off. Lay neatly in an ovenproof dish and sprinkle a little of the wine over it.
Beat the eggs, then add the remaining wine, salt, and sugar, then the saffron and almond milk. Mix together and pour over the bread.
Mix the spices together and scatter half over the top of the pudding.
Set the pudding dish in a large pan half-full of water and bake in a preheated oven at 350° for 25 minutes, or until set.
Sprinkle the top with the remaining ground spices and serve it forth.

SAFFRON SPICED TEA BREAD

A delicious tea bread that will keep for several days and makes excellent toast. It comes from the 1747 cookbook *The Art of Cookery Made Plain and Easy* by Hannah Glasse.

Makes 1 loaf

60 saffron filaments, or 1 packet of powdered saffron
3 tablespoons rose water
⅔ cup plus 1 generous tablespoon sugar
6 tablespoons warm water
1 packet active dry yeast

3 ¾ cups flour
½ teaspoon ground cloves
½ teaspoon ground mace
1 teaspoon ground cinnamon
2 eggs
¼ cup unsalted butter, gently warmed
⅔ cup milk

Combine the saffron and rose water. Heat, then leave to infuse for 1 hour. Dissolve 1 tablespoon of the sugar in the water and add the yeast. Stir until blended. Leave the mixture in a warm place for the yeast to activate.

In a large bowl combine the flour, the remaining ⅔ cup sugar, and the ground spices. Make a well in the center and add the eggs, yeast mixture, and the saffron rose water. Mix in well, then add the warmed butter and finally the milk. Knead in the bowl until the dough is smooth and elastic. Add more flour if needed. Cover the bowl with a warm cloth, then place in a warm place to rise for about 1 hour.

Punch the dough down, then place in an 8-inch greased cake pan and let rise until doubled in size.

Bake at 350° for 40 minutes. Cool on a rack before slicing.

ALMOND MILK

Almond milk was one of the basic cooking liquids in the Middle Ages. It can be made with milk or cream, or a mixture of the two, and can also have saffron added to it. I have substituted coconut milk on occasions where it is appropriate for a recipe. Orgeat Syrup is an almond-flavored sugar syrup (it is sweet) used by bartenders to make cocktails.

Scant 2 cups milk or cream
2 tablespoons ground almonds
¼ teaspoon almond extract

1 tablespoon orgeat syrup

Mix the ingredients together, then simmer for 10 to 15 minutes (do not boil). Allow to cool, then strain before use.

BRITAIN PAST
AND
PRESENT

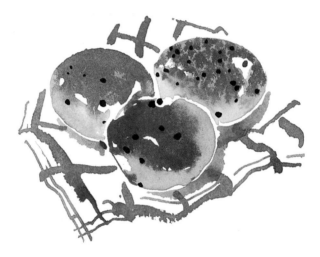

CORNWALL AS DEAR AS SAFFRON

Cornwall is the most southwesterly county of England, famous for ruby sunsets and golden saffron cakes. The peninsula is home to a cherished tradition of baking with saffron that dates from classical antiquity. Virtually every town will have a baker or tea shop offering bright yellow buns and cakes, displayed in baskets in shop windows. A cornish cream tea comprising the county's famed clotted cream, homemade jam, and saffron buns is, to my taste, far superior to the scones of neighboring Devonshire.

Lemon-colored soft buns and darkly crusted hard buns with a medium fruit content, currants, golden raisins, and sometimes chopped citrus peel, are widely available. Larger buns, known as "Tea Treats" or "Feast Buns," will often have a higher fruit content. Lightly toasted saffron tea cakes (wide flat buns) spread with rich Cornish butter are irresistible.

Cornish saffron cakes are baked in three sizes, usually "tin" or loaf-shaped, but some are round. All recipes contain yeast, are very fruity, and have a high fat content. Most often this is lard, with margarine used for a lighter textured cake. One baker uses butter, but only at Christmas time. The lard will preserve the cakes' freshness for up to three weeks. There is a delicious aroma in the bakery when the big oven door is opened and that morning's batch of saffron cake is removed.

So, how did this vibrant and enduring saffron tradition in Cornwall begin? Many other authors credit it to the Phoenicians, the great merchant sailors of the Mediterranean, yet they dismiss the possibility as myth or legend.

As discussed earlier, the Phoenicians were great traders of saffron and were the dominant power in the eastern Mediterranean from around 1000 B.C., when their realm of influence spread westwards. From around 850 B.C. their homelands came under increasing pressure from the Assyrians; as a result Tyre established a colony state in 814 B.C., on the north coast of Africa. It was called Carthage or "new city."

Carthage was able to protect and administer the Phoenician colonies in Sicily, Sardinia, Corsica, and in the south of France and Spain. In the century between 800 and 700 B.C., the foundation of Rome occurred, causing yet further problems for the Carthaginians. As a defensive measure, the Carthaginians blockaded the Straits of Gibraltar to protect and monopolize the tin trade they had established with Britain. Tin is found in Cornwall and was mined there commercially until very recent times.

Therefore, it is safe to assume that the Phoenicians/Carthaginians voyaged regularly to Cornwall for their supplies of tin. Here they would have bartered various products, including saffron, with the early British peoples. What I now find fascinating is that the memory of the golden-robed Phoenician sailors has endured for nearly 2,000 years.

Did the Romans then nurture this particularly West Country taste, and then was the baton passed to the church and abbeys or to the many saints the country embraced? Cornish seafarers traveled far and wide, possibly returning with cargoes of saffron or even a few corms for native cultivation during the Dark Ages. Could pilgrim monks traveling from Cornwall to the shrine of St. James in Santiago de Compostela on the Atlantic coast of Spain have kept the tradition alive, by returning with parcels of saffron to trade for their passage or accommodation, saffron being precious enough to be accepted as currency. In Tudor times, up to 20% of Saffron Walden's saffron crop was consumed in Cornwall. An old but still heard Cornish saying is "As dear as saffron."

CORNISH SAFFRON CAKES AND BUNS

Mrs. Mitchell of W. T. Warrens, bakers in St. Just, informed me that Warrens uses whole Mancha filaments, which are infused in hot water overnight. The whole solution, including the filaments, is added to the dough early in the morning. Warrens were founded in 1860 and have shops throughout Cornwall and a branch in Exeter in Devon, the most eastern outpost for Cornish saffron cake. They produce 7 tons of saffron cake each week. Recently Warrens have expanded their distribution from their West Country homeland, and their products are now found in London and elsewhere in Britain.

My favorite Cornish saffron cake is made by Blewetts of Truro, who also use whole filaments; the bright red strands are distinguishable in the warm yellow of the cake. Blewetts were founded in 1885 and have 3 shops in Truro, but recently they were taken over by Warrens. Two other bakers of note are W. C. Rowe of Penryn and Leslie Nile's of St. Austell.

Nowadays, when purchasing things, especially food, we need to be vigilant. We must buy only the best we can afford, and be aware of imitations. It is, therefore, disappointing to discover that many of the Cornish bakers supplement the saffron in their products with various kinds of yellow food colorants. Unfortunately E102, tartrazine and E110, sunset yellow are to be found among the ingredients, along with annatto and E100 curcumin (turmeric).

What brought about this debasement of such a noble food? In recent times two events combined to interrupt the supply of saffron to Cornwall: the Spanish Civil War, quickly followed by the Second World War. The bakers were forced to find alternatives. One of the wartime colorants was annatto, and the bad habit stuck. The growth of new food technologies since 1945 has produced a range of artificial colorants that the bakers have since made use of. When I questioned them about this, I was informed that it was unavoidable, an economic decision because of the cost of saffron. Yet the bakers buy saffron in vast kilo bales at very competitive prices, 10 or 20 pence worth of saffron is all that would be required in a cake that sells between $3 and $4.

I was also told, erroneously I believe, that a cake made only with saffron would be too strongly flavored for their customers, especially the important tourist trade. I suggest the bakers try us with a real saffron cake and see. The product is sold as "Saffron Cake" which is what I expect to buy, and not an "Azo Dye Cake."

A quality standard or purity law could be introduced to control the definition "Saffron Cake" administered by the local trading standards officers, in tandem with the Approved Origin Scheme which is already in place for products produced in Cornwall. There is, after all, an extremely long heritage to this particular Cornish speciality, which is worth cherishing.

Many autobiographies by Cornish people tell of their childhood enthusiasm for large saffron buns, served as a special treat at galas, Sunday school outings, and at Christmas. At a festive tea held to celebrate the Silver Jubilee, at Sincreed on May 6th, 1935, 40 pounds of saffron cake was supplied by Water Bros. of Newlyn at 8d a pound, a total of £1.6s.6d.

Noel Coward visited Charlesworth near St Austell in 1914, and later recalled the saffron cake as being "bright yellow and delicious" just as it is today.

The emigrant Cornish miners have spread their native saffron tradition world-wide, particularly in the last century. Several states in America—Wisconsin, Montana, Pennsylvania, Michigan, Nevada, and California—have pockets where the saffron tradition still flourishes. Also the Rand mines in South Africa and at Kaldoorlie in Western Australia. Even in the mining regions of North Wales in Britain, a different kind of a "gold rush," a herbal one, would be sent from home. The strong smell from the envelopes of saffron would arouse the suspicions of the local postal services. The miners' lunch boxes would also take on the saffron aroma, as a bun was often placed in a special compartment to be eaten as a "crib," a midmorning snack.

There is a record of saffron cultivation in Cornwall as late as the turn of the century. A "saffron field" near Penryn was sold by a medical man. In a book called *Neota*, privately published in 1871 by a Mrs. C. Hawkey, there is a reference to commercial cultivation at Launells near Stratton "for colouring the manifold cakes and Revel buns for which Launells was celebrated." The Cornwall Records Office has an old lease agreement dated December 1, 1653 for a saffron meadow at Fowey. The inventory of Francis Gregar, 1738, tells of a "saffron pot." In other documents there is mention of saffron meadows at Gerrans and Feoek. It is possible that saffron was cultivated at these sites. However, the word saffron being synonymous with yellow in the old Cornish dialect, could it have been another yellow crop, such as mustard or buttercups?

Several old Cornish books tell of bees becoming intoxicated after visiting a saffron crocus. I would think the bees' condition was more to do with the time of the year, which was late autumn. The bees were perhaps drowsy rather than drunk before their winter hibernation.

THE RECIPES

All of the Cornish saffron cake recipes I have seen require yeast but rarely eggs. They are in fact a kind of bread, rich and spiced. The high fruit, fat, and sugar content however is certainly of cake proportions. These golden, speckled loaves are a West Country variation of the traditional yeast cakes found in many other regions of Britain and Europe, enriched by the fruits and the distinctive presence of saffron's glow.

Many of the older recipes call for a sizeable quantity of saffron, up to ⅛ ounce (3.5 grams) for 2 pounds (1 kilogram) of flour. I can only assume that the compilers of these recipes from the 17th and 18th centuries were working with very poor quality saffron, as such a quantity of saffron would render a cake in modern times quite unpalatable and prohibitively expensive. Yet I have found that flour and the baking process absorb and dissipate saffron's flavor more readily than other ingredients. Therefore, I have portioned the saffron in the following recipes for flavor and aroma; color can be achieved with less. It is after all, a saffron-flavored cake that is being prepared, rather than merely a yellow one. If the recipes appear to be generous with the saffron, it is for reasons of flavor. I always use whole filaments when baking because I like to see them in slices of the finished cake, a sign that it has been made with the real thing.

Advanced preparation of the saffron was and still is recommended. The olden method was to place the filaments in a warm oven for five minutes to cure, before infusing overnight in water or milk, sometimes with a pinch of salt or sugar. The majority of the modern Cornish bakers use strong plain white flour, a bread flour; you may wish to use a softer flour in combination with it.

Have all the ingredients and utensils at room temperature or slightly warmer, 70 to 75 degrees. Mix all the dry ingredients together before adding the wet. I always sift the currants and raisins in a little dry flour before adding them to the mixture as a precaution against them sinking to the bottom of the cake during baking. For perfection and succulence, the fruits should be warmed or steamed for a few minutes before mixing in.

Air needs to be introduced to the mixture by kneading, until a smooth and elastic dough is formed, either by hand or in a food processor. The dough then needs time and the correct temperature to develop, the yeast to ferment, thus aerating the dough further and causing the mixture to rise. The proving (rising) of these fat rich mixtures is best done at a lower temperature than standard bread recipes, but for a longer time, around 1 hour or until the mixture has doubled in size.

Punching down the dough and doing a second kneading can be beneficial to the mixture. I find this so when using fresh yeast.

Oven temperatures need to be high to start with, then reduced for the final period. I place a ramekin of cold water in the bottom of the oven to improve the texture and crust of the cakes. For a final touch the dough can be "endored" immediately prior to being placed in the oven with a saffron and water wash, or a saffron and egg wash.

To be certain your cake is fully baked, rap it on the bottom with your fist. It should sound hollow. Insert a wooden toothpick; when removed, it should appear clean, without any of the cake sticking to it.

Finally, rest the cake for 1 hour before slicing. They are best when eaten freshly baked and just warm. The high fat content will retain the cake's freshness for a long period, up to 3 weeks if stored in a tin. It is recommended to put an older cake in a warm oven for a few minutes to restore its rich aromatic moistness.

Cornish bakers who supply saffron cakes by post are to be found on page 155.

ST. AUSTELL SAFFRON CAKE

4 teaspoons dry active yeast
6 cups flour
2½ cups warm milk
1 cup sugar
6 tablespoons lard
1 teaspoon salt (optional)

2 cups currants
2 cups mixed candied peel
100 saffron filaments, or 2 packets
    powdered saffron infused in hot
    milk overnight

Make a sponge by combining the yeast, 1 cup of the flour, 1 cup of warm milk, and 1 teaspoon of the sugar. Whisk together, then leave it to proof for 30 minutes.

Meanwhile, cut the lard into the remaining flour. Add the salt, the remaining sugar, and the currants and candied peel. When yeast is proofed and foamy, add it to the flour along with the rest of the warm milk and the saffron infusion. Knead well and leave to rise about 1 hour. Knead again then place the dough into greased baking tins and allow to rise for 30 minutes.

Preheat oven to 375° and bake for 30 minutes, then reduce heat to 225° and bake for 15 minutes. Allow to rest for 1 hour before slicing.

CORNISH SAFFRON BUNS

Makes 12 to 16

Prepare the dough as for the cake above. Then divide the dough into 4- to 6-ounce balls, mold into bun shapes, and place on a flat baking sheet. Allow the dough to rise 20 to 30 minutes before baking in a preheated oven at 375° for 12 to 15 minutes.

EXTRA RICH CORNISH SAFFRON CAKE

2 tablespoons dry active yeast
9 cups flour
2 ½ cups warm water
1 cup sugar
1 cup margarine
1 cup butter
¼ cup lard
2 teaspoons salt

2 cups mixed currants and yellow
  raisins
1 cup mixed candied peel (optional)
250 saffron filaments, or 4 to 5 packets
  powdered saffron infused in hot
  milk overnight
3 eggs

Make a sponge by combining the yeast, 1 cup of the flour, 1 cup of warm water, and 1 teaspoon of the sugar. Whisk together. Cover, then place in a warm place to allow the yeast to activate and the mixture to rise for 30 minutes to 1 hour. Rub the margarine, butter, and lard into the remaining 8 cups of flour. Add the salt, remaining sugar, and currants and candied peel. Add the saffron infusion and the eggs. Stir well, then add the sponge and enough warm water to make a soft dough. Knead well and leave to rise for 3 hours. Punch down, then knead again and put into greased baking tins to rise. Preheat the oven to 375° and bake for 30 minutes. Reduce heat to 300° and bake for 15 more minutes.

DEVONSHIRE SAFFRON CAKE

This is an interesting and somewhat rare recipe. It is the only one I know of that is entitled "Devonshire" and includes saffron. I found it in Elizabeth David's *English Bread and Yeast Cookery*; she in turn had found it in T. F. Garrett's *Encyclopedia of Practical Cookery*, published in 1899. The original recipe calls for that other West Country speciality: clotted cream. Heavy cream or butter can be substituted. E.D. recommends that the dough be left to rise overnight.

80 saffron filaments, or 1½ packets of powdered saffron infused in 1 tablespoon hot milk overnight
¼ ounce yeast
3 cups flour
2 cups heavy cream or butter
2 whole eggs

⅔ cup milk
1 ⅓ cups currants
1 teaspoon candied orange peel
¼ cup sugar
½ teaspoon salt
1 teaspoon Sweet Blend Spice (see below)

Prepare the saffron infusion, then dissolve the yeast with a little water. Warm the flour and stir in the cream and proofed yeast. Beat the eggs in the milk and add the saffron infusion.

Warm the currants and mix into the dough with the peel and sugar. Moisten the dough with the milk, egg, and saffron liquid, then add the salt and spice blend. The dough should be fairly stiff. Cover the bowl and leave in a warm place overnight to rise. Next morning, punch the dough down and knead it briefly.

Warm two cake tins and grease with butter. Split the dough between the tins, cover and allow the mixture to rise to the top of the tins, about 1 hour in a warm place. Bake in a preheated hot oven at 375°. Then cover the tops with paper and reduce the heat to 350° for 15 minutes more. Leave the cakes in their tins to cool for 10 minutes before turning them out onto a rack; let cool for about 1 hour before slicing.

ELIZABETH DAVID'S SWEET SPICE BLEND

This blend is published in *English Bread and Yeast Cookery*. Elizabeth based it on the "épices douces" from La Varenne's *Pastissier Francois* published in 1655.

Use two parts nutmeg; two parts white or black peppercorns (or for a milder blend two parts allspice berries); one part cinnamon stick; one part of whole cloves; one part of dried ginger. Crush and grind in a mortar and pestle. Use in hot cross buns, currant loaves, and puddings.

OTHER RECIPES FROM BRITAIN PAST AND PRESENT

 MUSSEL AND LEEK SOUP

This recipe was first published many years ago in a color supplement. In my dark age I would omit the saffron, but now this is one of my favorite recipes. It is from Rick Stein, of the Seafood Restaurant in Padstow, Cornwall.

Serves 4 to 6

3 pounds fresh mussels
3 tablespoons white wine
6 tablespoons butter
1 cup chopped leeks
1 small onion, chopped
¼ cup all-purpose flour

2 cups fish stock
40 to 50 saffron filaments, or 1 packet
   powdered saffron infused in
   3 tablespoons white wine
6 tablespoons heavy cream

Thoroughly wash the mussels, scraping off any barnacles. Discard any mussels that are gaping open and don't close up when given a good tap. Place them in a pan. Add a dash of the wine, cover, and cook over a high heat for about 5 minutes, shaking the pan until the mussels have opened. Strain the liquor through a colander into a bowl, shaking the colander well to drain off all the juice lodged in the shells. Melt the butter in a saucepan. Add the leeks and onion and soften them on a low heat in the butter for about 3 minutes. Add the remaining wine and let it reduce by half. Stir in the flour until smooth. Mix the mussel liquor with the fish stock and gradually add to the pan, stirring well. When the soup is smooth and simmering, add half the saffron infusion and cook for 25 minutes. Pull all the beards out of the mussels and discard one-half of each shell. Process the soup in a food processor and strain through a sieve into a clean saucepan. Reheat and stir in the remaining saffron, the cream, and the mussels on the half shell. Serve in warmed bowls.

SAFFRON PARSNIP SOUP

Saffron has a further affinity as well as the one with fish; root vegetables welcome saffron's influence to a very similar degree.

Serves 4

1 large onion, chopped
White part of 1 leek, chopped
½ carrot, chopped
3 garlic cloves, crushed
Extra virgin olive oil
2 pounds parsnips
5 ¼ cups vegetable or chicken stock
30 saffron filaments, or ½ packet
   of powdered saffron, infused
   in hot water

1 bay leaf
Crème fraîche
Unsalted butter
Salt and pepper

Garnish
Top-quality extra virgin olive oil
Chopped flat leaf parsley
Finely diced red bell peppers

Gently sweat together the onion, leek, carrot, and garlic in olive oil for 10 minutes. Meanwhile scrub, trim, and slice parsnips. Place parsnips in a separate saucepan with enough water to cover, bring to a boil for 2 minutes and reduce the heat and simmer. Add the stock and half the saffron infusion to the onion mixture, then add the bay leaf and simmer. When the parsnips are just soft, add them and their cooking water to the onion mixture. Mix together and simmer for 5 to 10 more minutes. Remove bay leaf. Then purée the mixture and return to pan over low heat. Fold in 2 dessertspoonfuls of crème fraîche and a pat of butter. Season to taste with salt and and pepper, then taste and adjust the seasonings. Add the remaining saffron infusion. Cook for 2 minutes more, stirring well. Garnish with a drizzle of extra virgin olive oil and the parsley and bell pepper. Serve in warm bowls with crusty bread.

SHELLFISH AND SAFFRON BROTH

A delicious broth from Frances Bissell's, *The Times Cook Book*.

Serves 4

3 pounds fresh mussels
1 pound prawns, in shells
1 small onion, peeled and halved
2 cloves
1 leek
Handful of parsley stalks
2 to 3 dill sprigs plus additional
   for garnish

1 teaspoon peppercorns
2 ½ cups dry white wine
⅔ cup water
1 carrot, shredded
30 saffron filaments or ½ packet
   powdered saffron infused in
   1 tablespoon of white wine
Freshly ground black pepper

Infuse the saffron in 2 to 3 tablespoons boiling water. Scrub the mussels, tug off the beards, knock off any barnacles with the back of a knife, and rinse throughly. Discard any that do not close. Put them in a bowl, and put to one side, reserving the shells. Put the prawn shells in a saucepan with the onion halves studded with the cloves. Trim and thoroughly wash the leek, cut it in half, and slice the green top half into rings. Add these to the saucepan, together with the parsley stalks, dill, peppercorns, wine, and water. Bring to a boil and simmer gently for 20 minutes. Meanwhile, peel the carrot (the carrot peeling can also go into the simmering broth), and cut into fine strips. Slice the bottom half of the leek lengthwise and shred in a similar fashion. Put these vegetables in a sieve, and pour boiling water over to soften them. Rinse under cold running water and put to one side.

Put the mussels in a heavy, lidded saucepan and pour the hot broth over them. Cover, bring to a boil, and simmer for 2 to 3 minutes, or just until all the mussels open. Discard any that fail to open. Carefully drain the broth into a clean saucepan through a sieve lined with muslin wrung out in hot water. When the mussels are cool enough to handle, remove them from their shells. Divide the prawns and mussels between heated soup plates, and scatter over them the carrot and leek shreds. Pour the saffron infusion into the broth, bring to a boil, and add pepper to taste. Pour into soup plates, garnish with the reserved dill, and serve at once.

SAFFRON FISH SOUP

The affinity between fish and saffron is readily appreciated. Possibly the greatest combination of the two is in a well-balanced fish soup. In reality, any fish soup recipe will be enhanced with the addition of saffron. I am grateful to Mary Griffiths of St. Alban's for sending me this recipe. To list a basic fish soup recipe without wandering off into countless variations and substitutions is impossible. Quite frankly, this recipe is more of a fish stew, a meal in a bowl, than it is soup. It provides a sound basis upon which you can elaborate, with shellfish or crab in the stock. You can also try vermicelli instead of potatoes.

Serves 4

3 large onions, finely chopped
1 leek sliced, white part only
6 garlic cloves, crushed
Olive oil
10 small new potatoes, scrubbed
5 ¼ cups fish stock
30 saffron filaments, or ½ packet
   powdered saffron, infused in
   3 tablespoons hot water

2 pounds firm white fish (such as
   halibut, turbot, eel, or haddock)
   filleted and cut into chunks (retain
   bones and heads for making stock)
Salt and pepper

Garnish
Cooked prawns
2 tablespoons chopped fresh parsley

Very gently sauté the onions, leek, and garlic in olive oil. Cook until the onion is soft, about 10 minutes. Stir and keep covered. Do not brown. Cut the potatoes into ¼-inch rounds and add to the onion mixture. Add more olive oil if needed. Cook on a low heat for 10 minutes. Add fish stock and half the saffron infusion. Mix well. Leave to simmer for 20 minutes. Taste; if no further reduction is required, add the fish and the remaining saffron infusion. Stir and simmer for a further 15 to 20 minutes. Check to be sure the fish is cooked and season with salt and pepper. Ladle into warmed bowls. Add a prawn or two for garnish and sprinkle with the chopped parsley.

CHORIZO AND RICE SOUP WITH SAFFRON

This is a warming, spicy, thick broth from Amanda Prichett, owner/chef of the busy Lansdowne pub/restaurant in London NW1.

Serves 4

2 onions, chopped
2 celery sticks, chopped
4 garlic cloves, chopped
3 tablespoons extra virgin olive oil
1 ½ teaspoons sweet paprika
10 cups light chicken stock
1 small bunch fresh thyme
2 bay leaves
2 cloves

1 whole spicy chorizo sausage
1 pound bacon
30 saffron filaments, or ½ packet of
   powdered saffron, infused in
   1 ½ tablespoons hot water
Salt and pepper
¾ cup short-grain rice

In a large saucepan, gently cook the onions, celery, and garlic in the oil until translucent. Stir in the paprika.

Add the stock, thyme, bay leaves, cloves, chorizo, and bacon. Simmer gently until the bacon is tender, for about 30 minutes. Remove the chorizo and bacon from the pan and slice them. Add the saffron infusion to the pan, then remove it from the heat. Season to taste with salt and pepper.

Bring the stock to a boil and add the rice 25 minutes before serving. Then simmer until soft, about 20 minutes. Put the sliced meats back in the pan and adjust the seasoning. Serve in warm bowls with crusty bread and additional extra virgin olive oil.

SAFFRON ICE CREAM

Adam Robinson, chef/proprietor of the excellent Brackenbury restaurant in West London, gave me this recipe. He serves this startlingly yellow ice cream with dark-colored fruit sorbets (blackcurrant or blackberry) for a dramatic visual effect.

Serves 2 to 4

2 ½ cups whole milk	5 egg yolks
¾ cup heavy cream	¾ cup sugar
20 saffron filaments, or ⅛ packet powdered saffron	

Bring the milk and the cream to a boil, add the saffron filaments, remove from heat, and leave to infuse overnight.

The following morning, beat the egg yolks and sugar in a bowl until smooth and white. Pour in a little of the saffron infusion and beat again.

Place the eggs mixture and the rest of the saffron infusion in a double boiler and cook over low heat for 3 minutes, or until the mixture coats the spoon.

Pass the mixture through a fine sieve, rescue the filaments from the sieve, return them to the mixture, and allow the mixture to cool. When cold, churn the mixture in an ice cream machine or chill in a bowl in the freezer. Remove at 1 hour intervals and beat it until it has set.

GOOSEBERRIES IN A HONEY SAFFRON CUSTARD

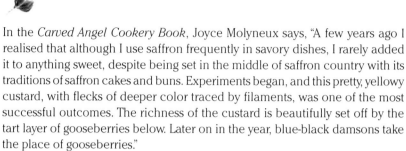

In the *Carved Angel Cookery Book*, Joyce Molyneux says, "A few years ago I realised that although I use saffron frequently in savory dishes, I rarely added it to anything sweet, despite being set in the middle of saffron country with its traditions of saffron cakes and buns. Experiments began, and this pretty, yellowy custard, with flecks of deeper color traced by filaments, was one of the most successful outcomes. The richness of the custard is beautifully set off by the tart layer of gooseberries below. Later on in the year, blue-black damsons take the place of gooseberries."

Serves 6

8 ounces fresh gooseberries, stemmed
  ¼ cup superfine sugar
3 tablespoons cold water
6 egg yolks
2 ½ cups cream

5 tablespoons delicate light honey
20 saffron filaments, or ⅛ packet of
  powdered saffron, infused in
1½ teaspoons hot water

Put the gooseberries into a pan with the sugar and water. Cover tightly and stew gently for 5 minutes, or until tender. Divide between 6 ramekins.

Whisk the egg yolks with the cream, honey, and saffron, and pour into a bowl set over a pan of simmering water, making sure that the base of the bowl does not touch the water. Cook the custard over a low heat for about 10 minutes, stirring until it is thick enough to coat the back of a spoon.

Strain the custard over the gooseberries in the ramekins. Stand the ramekins in a roasting tin filled with 1 inch of warm water. Bake in a preheated 275° oven for 45 minutes to 1 hour, or until just set. Serve warm or cold.

SAFFRON BREAD

From *The Complete Book of Spices* by Jill Norman.
Makes 1 large loaf

60 saffron filaments, or 1 packet powdered saffron	or ½ ounce dry active yeast
3 tablespoons hot water	¼ cup butter, melted
1 ¼ cups milk	4 tablespoons sugar
1 packet rapid-rising dry active yeast	½ teaspoon salt
	3 ¾ cups all-purpose flour

Steep the saffron in the hot water for 5 minutes.
Heat the milk. Pour off a little to cool to lukewarm and proof the yeast in it. Add the butter, sugar, and salt to the rest of the milk. Stir in the saffron and proofed yeast. If using rapid-rising yeast, mix directly into the flour. Add half the flour to the milk and beat well with a wooden spoon. Add the remainder gradually to make a shiny, cohesive dough. Knead the dough for 10 minutes, or until smooth and elastic. Put the dough in a lightly oiled bowl, cover with plastic wrap or a cloth. Leave to rise until it has doubled in bulk, about 1½ to 2 hours. Punch down, and form the dough into a loaf. Put the dough into a 2-pound buttered loaf tin, and leave to rise until it almost reaches the top.
Bake in a preheated oven at 425° for the first 10 minutes, then lower the temperature to 350° and bake for 15 to 20 more minutes. The loaf should sound hollow when tapped on the bottom.

QUICK SAFFRON BREAD

From *The Times Cook Book* by Frances Bissell.
Makes 1 large loaf or 8 to 10 rolls

30 saffron filaments or ½ packet powdered saffron	2 teaspoons salt
6 tablespoons boiling water	1 packet rapid-rising dry active yeast
4 ½ cups all-purpose flour	6 tablespoons extra virgin olive oil
	1 ¼ cups cold water

Put the saffron in a bowl and pour on a little boiling water. In a bowl or food processor, mix the dry ingredients and add all the liquids, including the oil and the saffron infusion. When it is thoroughly mixed, knead it for 10 minutes on a floured surface until smooth and elastic. Quickly shape it to fit your oiled loaf tin or baking sheet or divide into 8 to 10 small pieces. Shape these pieces into rounds and place on an oiled baking sheet. Cover with a damp towel, and leave to rise until doubled in volume. Bake in a preheated oven at 450° for 35 to 40 minutes if a large loaf (or 15 to 20 for rolls). Cool on a wire rack before slicing.

SAFFRON SCONES

A luxury tea-time treat. Serve with unsalted butter or clotted cream.

Makes 4 to 6 scones

1 ½ cups all-purpose flour
3 tablespoons baking powder
¼ teaspoons salt
⅔ cup raisins
¼ cup superfine sugar
¼ cup butter

20 saffron filaments or ⅕ packet
  powdered saffron, infused in
  1 tablespoon hot milk
⅔ cup milk

Sift the flour, baking powder, and salt into a large bowl. Add the raisins and sugar, mix together well, and then rub in butter.
Mix the saffron infusion into the ⅔ cup milk and reserve 2 tablespoons of the fluid. Mix the remaining milk and saffron into the flour to form a soft dough. On a floured surface, gently pat out the dough to about 1 inch thick. Divide the dough into 6 or 8 sheet pieces and brush with the remaining saffron-milk fluid. Transfer to a greased baking tray then place in a preheated 425° oven, for about 15 minutes or until golden brown. Remove from the oven and cool on the baking sheet.

SUNNY SAFFRON DUMPLINGS

From Rosemary Hemphill's *Herbs and Spices*. To be cooked in and served with rich winter stews.

Makes 8 to 10 dumplings

¼ cup milk
30 saffron filaments, or ½ packet
  powdered saffron
¾ cup self-rising flour

¼ teaspoon salt
¼ cup butter
2 teaspoons dried parsley or
  chopped fresh parsley

Heat the milk (do not boil) and add the saffron. Leave for 30 minutes to infuse. Sift the flour and salt in a bowl, rub in the butter, then mix in the parsley. Add the milk-saffron mixture to the flour and mix to form a stiff dough. Pat out on a floured surface and roll out lightly.
Divide the dough into small handfuls, and slash with a deep cut. Cook the dumplings in the stew for about 20 minutes with the lid on. Serve as soon as they are cooked.

SIMPLY SAFFRONED RICE

Serves 4

2 mugfuls of water
1 teaspoon salt
30 saffron filaments, infused in

3 tablespoons hot water or ½ packet
powdered saffron infused in
1 tablespoon of hot water
1 mugful of rice

Bring the water and salt to a boil. Add half of the saffron infusion and the rice. Cook until the water is absorbed and the rice is soft. Stir in the remaining saffron infusion and rest for 5 minutes before serving.

SAFFRON MASH

Simon Hopkinson was the head chef of Bibendum Restaurant in the old Michelin building in London. This recipe is found, with many others, in Simon's book, *Roast Chicken and Other Stories*.
My thanks to Simon for allowing me to use his original and now famous recipe, inspired by a lunch of bouillabaisse in the south of France. He recommends that if you serve these potatoes with fish, cook them in fish stock.

Serves 4

2 pounds potatoes, peeled
  and cut into chunks
Fish stock or water
Minimum 60 saffron filaments,
  infused in 3 tablespoons hot water
  or minimum 1 packet powdered
  saffron, infused in 3 tablespoons
  hot milk

1 large garlic clove, peeled and
  finely chopped
¾ cup whole milk
¾ cup virgin olive oil
Tabasco sauce to taste
Salt and black pepper

Boil potatoes in fish stock or water with some salt.
Heat together saffron, garlic, and milk. Cover and leave to infuse for 10 minutes. Add olive oil to milk mixture and gently reheat.
Drain and mash potatoes, place in the bowl of a mixer, switch on, and add saffron milk in a steady stream. Add Tabasco to taste and adjust seasoning. Allow purée to sit in a warm place for about 30 minutes so the flavors develop.

SAFFRON CREAM DRESSING

My thanks again go to Simon Hopkinson for this recipe. He recommends serving this with white crabmeat or lobster, prawns, or scallops.

60 saffron filaments or 1 packet
  powdered saffron, infused
  in 3 tablespoons boiling water
½ lemon, juiced
Pinch of salt

Pinch of cayenne
1 teaspoon smooth Dijon mustard
Scant ¾ cup heavy cream

Infuse the saffron for 30 minutes, then mix together with the lemon juice, salt, cayenne, and mustard. Allow the mixture a few minutes to develop, then blend in the cream and serve straight away.

SAFFRON HADDOCK

This is an adaptation of a medieval recipe by Fergus Henderson, a partner and head chef at the St. John restaurant in Smithfield, London.

Serves 2

1 large glass dry white wine
2 teaspoons Colman's mustard powder
Splash of water
Salt and pepper
Dash of oil

2 natural smoked haddock fillets
30 saffron filaments, or ½ packet
  powdered saffron, infused in
  3 tablespoons white wine
Pat of butter

Mix together the rest of the wine, mustard, water, salt, and pepper. In an oven-proof pan heat the oil and briefly fry the haddock. Pour in the wine mixture and saffron infusion. Bubble together for 1 minute. Put the pan into a hot oven for 10 minutes. When the haddock is cooked, reserve on a warm plate. Return the pan to the flame to reduce wine and cooking juices. Add the pat of butter so the sauce binds. It will become rich and delicious. Pour over the haddock and serve.

FRAGRANT KEDGEREE

Ian Ellison of Shropshire kindly sent me this recipe. He recommends it for a weekend breakfast.

Serves 4

1 pound thick wood-smoked
  haddock fillets, skin on
2 ½ cups cold water
6 tablespoons butter
1 small onion, thinly sliced
½ teaspoon ground cumin
¼ teaspoon chile powder
3 tablespoons golden raisins
1 mugful basmati rice

30 saffron filaments, or ½ packet
  powdered saffron, infused in
  1 tablespoon hot water
1 teaspoon ground coriander seeds
3 hard-boiled eggs, sliced
3 tablespoons chopped parsley
1 tablespoon lemon juice
Salt and freshly ground black pepper

Place haddock fillets in a pan and cover with the cold water. Bring to a boil, put on lid, and simmer very gently for 5 minutes (do not boil). Drain off cooking liquid and reserve. Transfer haddock to dish, cover, and keep warm.

Using the pan used to cook the haddock, melt two-thirds of the butter and gently fry onion, without browning, for 5 to 10 minutes until pale golden yellow and soft. Stir in the coriander, cumin, chile powder, and golden raisins; cook for 1 minute. Add the breakfast mug of unrinsed basmati rice. Stir and heat for 2 minutes. Add saffron infusion and a mugful of the cooking liquid. Stir once and bring to boil, then reduce to gentle simmer. Cover with tight fitting-lid and cook for 15 minutes.

While rice is cooking, remove skin from haddock fillets and coarsely flake fish. When rice is ready, gently fold in flaked haddock, hard-boiled eggs, parsley, lemon juice, and the rest of the butter.

Cover pan with a towel and heat very gently for 5 minutes more. Transfer to a hot serving dish, season with salt and black pepper, and serve hot.

SAFFRON VINAIGRETTE

This is one of my favorite and one of the most adaptable saffron recipes. Use this gilded vinaigrette on salad leaves or with fish and shellfish. To have saffron vinaigrette available at all times, I have developed the following shortcut.

80 to 100 saffron filaments, powdered,
  or 2 packets powdered saffron
15 to 20 saffron filaments
1 bottle white wine vinegar

Mild and fruity extra virgin olive oil
  or neutral tasting salad oil
Salt and pepper
Lemon juice

Empty the white wine vinegar into a large saucepan. Retain the bottle. Add the powdered saffron and heat to just below boiling point, for 1 minute. Cool, then add the 15 to 20 filaments and return the vinegar to its bottle. Let it stand overnight. To make saffron vinaigrette with the saffron vinegar, add either a mild and fruity extra virgin olive oil or a neutral tasting salad oil. Use one part vinegar to six parts oil. Add salt and pepper to taste.

As with any basic vinaigrette, adaptations can be made with the addition of a few drops of sherry vinegar, lemon, lime, or orange juice, or a little Colman's mustard powder.

Extra saffron can be incorporated, if desired, either in powdered form or by gently warming filaments and steeping them in lemon juice or a little vinegar for 10 minutes before adding to the oil mixture.

A little clear honey, rosemary, or lavender can be added if the acidity of your vinaigrette is too strong, but it is best to warm the honey first.

Allow time for the flavors to develop.

Saffron vinegar is a useful liquid to have at hand (and a shortcut on the infusion process). It can be added to any recipe that calls for vinegar.

SAFFRON HOLLANDAISE

I cheat when I make hollandaise and make it in a blender, having discovered an American recipe many years ago which said, "this hollandaise never fails." It never has.

30 saffron filaments or ½ packet powdered saffron infused in lemon juice
1 to 2 generous tablespoons lemon juice

4 egg yolks
¼ teaspoon salt
Pepper
1 cup unsalted butter

Bring all ingredients to room temperature.

First, mix the saffron filaments and lemon juice and leave for 30 minutes before commencing. Next, fill the blender with hot water. Leave it to warm the jar for a few minutes. Empty the water into a saucepan over low heat. Stand the blender jar in the saucepan and put the egg yolks, lemon juice–saffron infusion, salt, and a couple of grinds of fresh black pepper in the jar. After 5 minutes, gently combine this mixture, then return the blender jar to the saucepan to keep warm. Meanwhile slowly heat the butter until hot and bubbly and stir. Return the blender jar to the motor base. Turn to a slow beat and start to add the hot butter, slowly at first, and then in a steady stream. The hollandaise will form in front of your eyes; taste to check seasoning. Be watchful, you may not need all the butter. If the sauce is too thick, thin by adding a little hot water or more lemon juice.

For the double boiler method of making hollandaise: steep the powdered saffron in lemon juice and/or vinegar for 20 minutes, then proceed in the normal way. But beware: saffron filaments will entwine themselves in your whisk, so add whole filaments at the end by gently stirring in with a spoon. Whole filaments can be used in either of these recipes to add hot spots of color and texture to your sauce.

SAFFRON MAYONNAISE

I rarely make mayonnaise from scratch nowadays. The 20 minutes or so that it takes to make by hand is too time consuming. Therefore, for convenience, I prefer to enhance store-bought prepared mayonnaise.

30 saffron filaments, powdered, or ½ packet powdered saffron

6 tablespoons mayonnaise

For instant saffron mayonnaise, combine the saffron and prepared mayonnaise to make a deep yellow emulsion speckled with tiny red dots. Preparation time is 3 minutes maximum!

30 saffron filaments, powdered or ½ packet powdered saffron
10 saffron filaments for garnish

Dash of lemon juice or white wine vinegar
6 tablespoons mayonnaise

For a mayonnaise with a greater saffron flavor it is best to steep the saffron in a few drops of lemon juice or white wine vinegar for 30 minutes, then mix together with the back of a teaspoon, and combine into the sauce. Taste for seasoning. More oil can be incorporated if required. Sprinkle the 10 whole filaments over the mayonnaise, leaving no doubt as to its magical ingredient.

SAFFRON SAUCE FOR SEAFOOD AND FISH

I always make this sauce with powdered saffron as it needs to be strained. Nothing is worse than having precious saffron filaments entwined in the mesh of a strainer. I add some infused filaments after straining for decoration and extra saffron flavor.

15 saffron filaments,
    or ¼ packet powdered saffron
1 cup white wine
2 tablespoons unsalted butter
2 medium shallots, finely chopped

⅔ cup fish stock
3 tablespoons heavy cream
    or crème fraîche
10 saffron filaments whole, infused
    in 1 tablespoon white wine

Powder the 15 filaments and steep in the wine for 20 minutes. Melt the butter, add the shallots and sauté, but do not allow them to brown. Add the fish stock and the wine–saffron infusion. Simmer gently for 10 to 15 minutes. Taste the broth; it may need extra reduction to increase flavor. (Extra "fishiness" can be induced by judicious use of anchovy purée, but be careful of the salt content.) When satisfied, strain the broth and return to the pan. Fold in the cream or crème fraîche and heat to serving temperature. Decorate with 10 or so previously infused filaments, and serve from a warmed sauceboat. This sauce can also be poured over grilled fish and then browned under the already hot grill.

SPAIN

Harvest La Mancha

My saffron safari began on October 28, 1993, when I turned the keys of a rental car at Valencia airport and headed inland along the N111. My first destination was the town of Requena where I had a meeting with one of my wine suppliers. It was a little odd to be in a wine town a month or so later than normal; previously I would have visited in September to witness the grape harvest. The meeting over, I traveled on through the ruby and bronzed vineyards, already dormant. I was in search of other treasure. I headed south and west on the N322 to the town of Albacete where I was to meet Sr. González from Safinter and his party at the Parador hotel.

We met at dinner, 4 Swedes, 3 Spaniards, 2 Italians, and 1 Englishman, and enjoyed a delicious meal of regional specialities: tiny piquillo peppers stuffed with veal and vegetables, followed by "Perdiz Estofado" (see page 91), stewed partridge with a complex earthy sauce, the autumnal flavor being emphasised with just a little saffron. We drank a surprisingly good La Mancha Tinto and finished with the local, and my favorite of all the Spanish cheeses, Manchego. My Swedish dinner companions provided me with much information on saffron. One was an importer, another the spice buyer of a large supermarket chain. We postponed further conversation as an early night was required to prepare us for a dawn start the following day.

The morning was cold and gray. However, the monotone was soon to be banished by my first sight of a saffron garden. It was the most vivid hue of regal purple. Even from a distance, the fiery red of the stigmas could be seen, dancing gently in the breeze.

The *celamina* (saffron garden) was the size of two tennis courts. I walked from the car and squatted down at the end of the rows. It was difficult to comprehend, to face this abundant colorful reality, that the simple beauty of flowers could produce such a complex substance as saffron. Further to my right, the Gomez family toiled, stooped low to pick the garland crop. Each flower head, still closed, was placed into esparto grass baskets dangling from the pickers' waists. Monet would have triumphed with this scene.

I was awestruck. For a minute or two I could only sit and stare at what was before me: a scene not unfamiliar throughout the history of mankind, in fact the reverse. I was witnessing something that had occurred in Spain every autumn for the last one thousand years, possibly longer.

I joined in and picked my first crocus. I was astonished at the amount of yellow dye on my hand from rubbing the wet stigmas between my fingers. But as yet no saffron aroma or flavor; these are revealed after the wet stigmas are cured (dried). A good-sized fresh stigma is something like a bean shoot, but red. I labored with the family for half an hour. I have no doubt it is back-breaking work. Our need to move on brought my agony to an end. We headed for the nearby town of Balazote, where Sr. González needed to inspect the previous day's crop which had been dried by Sr. Gomez Senior, now too old to join the rest of the family in the fields. We entered into the small hallway of the grower's house. Sr. González and Sr. Gomez embraced and exchanged warm greetings. They had been doing business together for over 50 years. There, spread on the table, were the limp bruised crocus petals and, in radiant contrast beside them, was a crimson pile of dried stigmas: saffron. A set of very ancient scales was produced, but both grower and buyer were happy to use them, as they had for the last 5 decades. We left them to discuss their business. Soon Francisco, Sr. González's production manager, was loading a 2-kilo sack in the back of the car.

We moved on westwards through the villages of Lezuza and El Bonillo. We passed by many more crocus plantations, and, curiously, the occasional daub of discarded crocus petals, now blueish and certainly forlorn. Some growers believe that it is unlucky to take the crocus flowers home, so they pluck the wet stigmas from the flowers by the side of the road. Despite various attempts, no practical use has yet been found for the petals.

Our destination that day was the Parador Hotel at Manzanares, which is quite a famous wine town, but just down the road is Valdepeñas, the jewel of La Mancha wine making. I had a few spare hours so I went on a tasting tour of some of the bodegas.

The next morning, our foray into saffron country was all of 300 meters from the hotel to a very large flat field that stretched to the horizon. It was covered by a mantle of purple, a sea of saffron. The wind was strong and, combined with the broken sunlight, gave the impression of a wavelike motion. The mirage was complete; the Manzanares is about as land locked as one can be in Spain. The line of the horizon was interrupted, mastlike, by the occasional tree, and when a picker stood upright, to ease their back for a few seconds.

Near where we had parked the cars was a gully with mounds cut from its sides. The mounds had doors in them, and to our amazement, people living behind the doors. We were invited in by an eccentic old woman. Her "cave" was cozy and dry, and had several windows at the front and a fireplace in each room. Stepping out of her dwelling, I could see the telecommunication and television aerials of the town. That step seemed to span a thousand years.

We moved on to the other side of town. Through an open door I caught the scent I had been expecting; it was saffron drying. We entered the house; in a corner grouped around a table were eight women, the *mondadoras*, or peelers, some of whom were dressed in the traditional black clothes. They were diligently working their way through a huge pile of crocus flowers; an experienced *mondadora* can remove the stigmas from up to 10,000 flowers in a day. In La Mancha this is called the *pelanda*, and is laborious and delicate work. I was again shocked by the colors, not the colors of food, but of stained glass: a hillock of purply blue in the center, on top of what had earlier been a white tablecloth. The *mondadoras'* hands were now blue from handling the flowers. In front of them were white tin plates piled high with the brilliant red stigmas, a halo of yellow encircling each plate.

An old woman shuffled in, carrying something like a garden sieve. Silently she moved around the table, tipping the contents of the tin plates into her sieve. I followed her to a large fireplace, where charcoal embers were glowing. Carefully placing the sieve on a metal rack, the drying began. Periodically, she would give it a shake and stir. This process is know as *tueste*. As the stigmas dry, the air is filled, slowly at first, with the distinctive aroma of top-quality La Mancha saffron. It is smoky yet fresh, deeply pungent, earthy, exotic, yet familiar. I inhaled deeply and was immediately hungry.

Sr. González played a joke on me by announcing we were having gazpacho for lunch. Although delicious on a hot day, it was not what I was expecting for lunch on a cold day in late October. He had omitted a word—Manchego—which is quite another dish. It is served hot with pasta, strangely broken from large flat sheets. The broth in this case was partridge-based. We all agreed it was first class.

That evening saw our arrival at Almargo, at possibly the most beautiful Parador in all of Spain, which was once an old monastery and is certainly within one of the most attractive towns. As we checked in and our collective aroma preceded us, the receptionist said immediately, "azafran!" The party of Safinter, Welcome. Almargo is the home of the unique Corral de Comedias, an old, wooden, galleried theater built in Shakespearean times. There is an unusual Flemish influence in the Plaza Mayor.

The following morning we were joined by a group of English journalists, shepherded by Maria José Sevilla, from the Spanish Government Agency, Foods from Spain. It was good to meet with them all and discuss our experiences of La Mancha.

It was the last Sunday in October and therefore the day of XXXI Fiesta de la Rosa del Azafran, in Consuegra, Spain's saffron capital. Consuegra is the town that embodies all that is La Mancha. There are ten windmills and a castle high on the ridge above the town, a picture that is found in every travel guide. This is Don Quixote country. Our journey from Almagro was due north, directly across the empty plain where vast horizons and even larger sky diminish every other feature.

By contrast, Consuegra was packed. The fiesta was in full swing. We headed for the town hall past crowds of people dressed in traditional costume, each wearing a crocus on their lapel. We were there to witness a saffron-plucking competition. A bag with one hundred flowers is placed before the contestants. When the judges give the word, the plucking starts. The winner is the one to finish first. It was very close and quite exciting. I saw money changing hands later; there had been some betting at the back of the hall.

The festivities concluded with a concert and dance, which, because of the rain, was held in the local sports hall and not in Consuegra's town square. Bands and dancers of all ages from the surrounding villages would take turns entertaining the throngs of people and later the entire nation, as there were several television crews filming.

It was the very essence of Spain: stamping feet set the rhythm, accented by the sharp incessant retort of castanets. The lace headresses of the girls swirled as they were spun by their aloof partners. The guitars strummed the open chords of flamenco. We clapped, cheered, and joined in the dance.

Maria José's party had to depart for Madrid airport. Goodbyes said, our group headed north to Toledo, once the capital of Spain and an old and dignified city, whose Moorish influence is still evident in the renowned marzipan the city produces.

There were more goodbyes to be said that evening after dinner, as our safari in saffron country had come to an end.

The next morning I retraced my journey, returning east across the plain. I left behind me the still-visible purple patches of crocus plots. I passed by sheep, roadside cheese shops, windmills, and castles. There were millions of stumps of ground-hugging vines, kept low to protect them from the wind and heat, their countless rows meeting before fading over the horizon. I left La Mancha for Valencia by turning onto the N111, "the road to the sea", from Madrid. I was heading back to Requena, once a major silk town. The textile trade has provided a ready market for the neighboring saffron growers for many centuries. I was to meet Felix Martinez at his bodega, Casa Don Angel, for lunch.

We toured the Utiel Requena DO wine region during an afternoon of sun, rain, and rainbows, but much warmer than up on the higher plain of La Mancha. Near to Casa del Pinar, the bodega owned by London restaurateurs Philip and Anna Diment, I shouted "stop the car," for I had seen at the bottom of a valley the purple haze of a crocus plantation. Felix and I investigated. By now it was 5 o'clock in the afternoon and, despite signs of some harvesting, it seemed that this saffron was being left ungathered. The stigmas were long and contained as much yellow dye as I had encountered in La Mancha.

We finished our day at a restaurant in El Palmar on the shores of the Albufera lagoon. We shared a bottle of Felix's delicious Vina Carmina, a rosado made from the local Bobel grape with a huge "Arroz a Banda," saffron seafood rice as yellow as a beacon.

LA MANCHA — THE QUALITY FACTOR

Castilla La Mancha, to give it its full title, straddles the geographic center of Spain. It is composed of 5 provinces: Albacete, Ciudad Real, Cuenca, Guadalajara, and Toledo.

The main saffron production extends over the central plateau, the *Meseta*, at an elevation of 1,000 meters. It stretches from Albacete in the east to Toledo in the west, from Cuenca in the north and Valdepeñas in the south.

Because of the altitude, the climate is extreme, conditions in which saffron thrives, similar to Kashmir and Iran. In summer, the temperature will soar above 40°C for many months. In winter it will fall below freezing.

The soil is composed of gravel, chalk, and clay. The loam is light. There is no shade over the saffron fields. To the growers, saffron is a cash crop demanding relatively little of their time, just 7 to 10 working days a year.

Their *Suerete* will need to be well hoed and fertilized during the spring, mainly with manure. The corms are planted in June or July. Their plot needs to be kept weed-free during the growing period. Come October, the real work commences — the *cosecha* or harvest. Each plant will flower up to three times. The number of crocus grown by the farmer will be limited by how much his family can harvest during the brief season. It has been calculated that 400 hours are needed to produce 1 kilo of saffron. In recent years, the yield per hectare (2.4 acres) has been increased because of improved corm selection and irrigation. Up to 25kg can now be produced by each hectare.

The crop from 160,000 crocus flowers will yield 5 kilos of wet stigmas, which will then reduce to 1 kilo when dried. In other words, it takes the stigmas from 5,200 flowers to make one ounce (28.5 grams). The 40 filaments in one of my recipes will be the harvest of 14 flowers. Need you wonder why saffron is so costly?

It is curious that this prized spice is produced in the poorest and, often,in the most arid regions in the world. Production is a family affair, where the extra income a few kilos will provide is most welcome. The export value is worth millions to the Spanish economy and yet, in several guides to La Mancha I have read, containing specialist chapters on the gastronomy of the region, saffron is not mentioned. Perhaps the authors of these books visited the region in months other than October, thereby failing to record the cultivation of this purple cloak of herbal gold.

PAELLA: PAN, DISH, AND CULTURE

The Moors introduced the cultivation of rice into Spain; together with their passion for saffron, they created the foundation of the world's greatest rice feast: paella. The Romans also played their part, by establishing irrigation systems, improved by the Moors, and by developing the flat cooking pot that would evolve into the present-day paella pan.

Just south of Valencia is a freshwater lagoon, La Albufera (meaning "little sea" in Arabic), which is where the Moors located their paddy fields. The lagoon teems with fish, especially eels. The surrounding hills and mountains, famous for their orange trees, are also the principal market-garden of Spain and the habitat of many game animals. The proximity of the Mediterranean, with its abundant supply of fish and shellfish, has further contributed to the stock of the local chefs' larders with good ingredients to add to the rice of these celebrated dishes.

Paella Valenciana is principally a (short grain) rice dish; the authentic version does not have fish or shellfish in it. It is made with chicken, rabbit, and beans. It should also be cooked on a wood fire, preferably with vine cuttings, in the open air. The smoke from a wood fire curls over the low rim of a paella pan, adding a further flavor to the rice. I thank my friends, the Martinez family, wine growers of neighboring Requena, for taking the trouble to cook such a paella for me.

Arroz a la Marinera and Arroz a Banda are the names of the golden yellow seafood and rice combinations so famous throughout the world. They are cooked in a paella pan but they are not paella Valenciana. Seafood paella is an incorrect but widely used term.

However, all is not what it seems in this plentiful region, for many of the local restaurants make false and fraudulent economies by not using saffron in the rice. They use the truly awful chemical food dye called "colorante" or "paella powder," which is in fact *tartracina*, E102. When one considers the cost of lobsters or prawns, to corrupt the dish for the sake of a few extra pesetas worth of real saffron is mean and a gastronomic rip-off. Especially as these restaurateurs can buy saffron more cheaply than anyone else in the world. It grows in the Valencia region, and the vast store of saffron in La Mancha is only one hour's drive away.

People in London also suffer a similar fate with their Spanish restaurants. The proprietors, who are mainly Galicians, are not known for their love of saffron. They claim the English do not like the taste of saffron. Yet they are ignorant of our own saffron heritage. A tortilla cannot be made without breaking eggs, likewise paella-style dishes without real saffron are a destitution. If you order a paella, demand to see the saffron before they start cooking it; when it is served, check for the long red filaments in the rice. If absent send it back. They will soon get the right idea if this happens often enough.

There follows a list of tips and suggestions to ensure you can prepare successful and delicious paella recipes at home.

1. Use only real saffron infused for an hour or so and added to the rice during the last third of the cooking time.
2. I prefer not to mix meat and seafood; some people like to see chicken with fish. It is a question of taste.
3. Use only short- or round-grain rice, preferably Spanish; Italian can be substituted. Short-grain rice has a much higher starch content than long grain. The starch soaks up, like a sponge, all the flavors within the recipe. Once I used pudding rice from a supermarket and it produced a good paella, much better than could be achieved with regular long-grain rice.
4. Many English cooks find it curious to fry the rice before adding the cooking liquid. I assure you it is absolutely necessary to do so.
5. The cooking liquid can be water. Some purists in Spain will argue it gives the best results with certain paella recipes. The more flavor the cooking liquid has, the more will be imparted to the rice—I like to use a very strong crab-based stock and then use crabmeat and claws in the final presentation.
6. Paella pans are not expensive, especially if you buy one in Spain while on vacation. The best and cheapest place to do so is in the Mercado Central in Valencia. They come in a range of sizes. A paella pan with a diameter of 16 inches is the right size for 4 people. Spanish paella pans will often rust after washing, therefore it is best to oil them to prevent this, then wipe the oil off with a paper towel before reusing. You can use any other large, shallow, flat–bottomed pan, even a roasting tin. What is important is that the rice can be spread out thinly, no deeper than ½ inch to ensure even cooking.
7. With such a large pan it can be difficult to get an even heat. Be prepared to use more than one burner and turn the pan frequently. Purists insist that the rice should not be stirred. This is to encourage the formation of a *socarrat*, a golden crust of rice, crunchy and flavorsome, that forms at the edges and bottom of the pan. For *socarrat* we could read *tahdeeg*, from the Persian, for they are both the crunchy layer of rice that forms on the bottom of the pan of unstirred rice. The Moors (Arabs) learned their rice cooking skills from the Persians and then introduced their love for the crunchy crust to Spain over one thousand years ago.
8. The final cooking of the rice, the swelling of the grains, happens off the heat while the paella is resting. Be watchful not to overcook it. In Spain, paella is served at room temperature rather than hot.
9. Suppliers of paella pans can be found in Appendix IV.

PAELLA VALENCIA

Serves 4 to 6

⅔ cup plus 2 tablespoons
   extra virgin olive oil
1½ pounds chicken, in small pieces
1 pound rabbit pieces or lean pork
4 ounces fresh green beans
1 tomato peeled, and finely chopped
1 teaspoon Spanish paprika
8 ¾ cups hot water
12 snails (optional)
Salt

1 large sprig rosemary
2 ⅔ cups short-grain rice
40 to 50 saffron filaments, or 1 packet
   powdered saffron, infused in
   3 tablespoons hot water
1 large can butter beans, drained

Heat the oil in a paella pan (or a large swallow frying pan or roasting pan). Fry the chicken and rabbit pieces until evenly browned. Reduce the heat and add the green beans and tomato. (Onions and garlic can also be used if desired; they should be chopped and fried along with the beans and tomato). Fry for 2 minutes, then add the paprika and 4 ½ cups of the water. Bring to a boil, then reduce the heat and simmer until the meat is cooked, about 45 minutes.

Add the snails and rosemary, check the seasoning, and add salt if required. Add the saffron infusion, the remaining 4 ½ cups of the water, and butter beans, bring to a boil. Add the rice and cook at a high temperature for 10 minutes. Be sure to spread the rice evenly in the pan and stir only once. Reduce the heat and simmer until the rice is just ready and the water has been absorbed, 8 to 10 more minutes. Remove from the heat and cover the pan to allow the paella to rest before serving on warm plates.

Note: You may prefer to skin the chicken and/or marinate it in red wine for a few hours for additional color and flavor.

ARROZ A LA MARINERA
FISH AND SEAFOOD RICE COOKED IN A PAELLA PAN

You need to make 5 to 7 ½ cups of fish stock for this recipe. For the fish, choose from monkfish, hake, whiting, sea bream, scorpion fish, eel, halibut, etc. Your fishmonger may be able to provide you with fish heads, bones, and scraps. Serves 4 to 6

FISH STOCK

9 tablespoons olive oil
1 pound fish
1 large onion, chopped
1 tomato, peeled and chopped
10 ½ cups water
1 teaspoon paprika

Prawn shells and heads, crushed
Shrimp shells and heads, crushed
Lobster shells and heads, crushed
Crab shells, crushed
Crayfish shells and heads, crushed

Heat the oil in a large pan and briefly fry the chosen fish. Remove and set aside. In the same oil, fry the onion and tomato. Combine the fried fish and onion and tomato in a large saucepan with the water and paprika and shellfish shells, which have been broken down and crushed. Cover and cook over medium heat for 20 minutes, then strain through a fine sieve and keep warm.

THE RICE

9 tablespoons olive oil
1 tomato, peeled and chopped
1 garlic clove, finely chopped
Fish stock (see recipe above)
2 ⅔ cups short-grain Spanish rice
30 saffron filaments, or ½ packet
   powdered saffron infused in
   3 tablespoons hot water

Mussels on half shell, clams on half
   shell, crayfish, prawns, shrimp,
   squid in rings, lobster tails and
   claws, or cooked and cleaned
   crab claws
1 lemon, cut into wedges

Heat the oil in a paella pan and gently fry the tomato and garlic for 5 minutes. Bring the fish stock to a boil. Add the rice to the paella pan and fry for 5 minutes, ensuring each grain is coated with oil. Add the saffron infusion and stir. Increase the heat and add half the boiling fish stock and stir. Cook at a high temperature for 10 minutes as required. Do not let the rice dry out or burn. Add more stock if needed. Taste the rice to check how well it's cooked. Start to add the shellfish and stir. When the rice is tender yet al dente, remove it from the pan and let it rest for 5 minutes. Serve with the lemon wedges.

RISOTTO LA MANCHA

I believe this to be an original recipe, based firmly on a traditional one, but born at the last moment, when a vital ingredient was missing. In this case, the missing ingredient was Parmesan cheese. It is said by several other authors that risotto evolved from paella, Italy being under Catalan rule during the early Middle Ages. If so, risotto has now come full circle and returned home. I substituted manchego for the Parmesan. The final last-minute ingredient change was the addition of some fresh English peas. This "new" creation was, I admit, delicious.

Serves 4 to 6

1 medium onion, finely chopped
2 shallots, finely chopped
3 cloves garlic, crushed
   and finely chopped
2 tablespoons extra virgin olive oil
   plus a dash
2 ounces pancetta, diced
2 ⅔ cups Spanish round-grain rice
30 saffron filaments, or ½ packet
   powdered saffron, infused
   in a glass of white wine

4 ½ cups homemade ham stock, warm
   Fresh English peas, blanched, or
   a little chopped flat-leaf parsley
2½ cups unsalted butter
2 ounces grated Manchego cheese

Note: Use arborio rice if you cannot find the Spanish rice.
Gently fry the onion, shallots, and garlic in the olive oil. Do not brown. Start to add the pancetta, stirring it well. Let the fat cook out of the ham, add the dash of olive oil, and stir in the rice. Stir to coat every grain of rice, then gently fry for 5 minutes. Increase heat a little, add the wine-saffron infusion, reserving a little. When the wine is absorbed, start to add hot stock by the ladleful and allow it to cook off before adding the next. Four or five ladles may be needed. Keep stirring to prevent the rice from sticking. Taste rice after about 15 minutes—it should be creamy but al dente. Stir in the peas and remaining saffron. Remove from the heat. Stir in the butter and Manchego cheese. Cover and let rest for 3 minutes. Serve in warm bowls.

CHICKEN AL ANDALUS

This is an old recipe from Castile, with a strong Moorish influence.

Serves 6

6 tablespoons olive oil	½ teaspoon ground cinnamon
1 thick slice of bread	½ teaspoon ground cloves
2 garlic cloves, crushed	30 saffron filaments, dry-fried,
10 almonds, chopped	or ½ packet powdered saffron
3 pounds chicken pieces	½ teaspoon cumin seeds
1 large onion, finely chopped	2 hard-boiled egg yolks
2 ½ cups water	Salt
1 teaspoon lemon juice	

Heat the oil in a deep casserole and fry the bread, garlic, and almonds for a few minutes and remove. Then sauté the chicken pieces; when golden, remove and set aside. In the same oil, fry the onion until soft. Return all of the above, except the almonds, to the casserole. Cover with the water, and add the lemon juice, cinnamon, and cloves. Cover and cook on a low heat for 1 hour.

Place the saffron in a mortar with the almonds and cumin seeds. Crush this mixture, then add the egg yolks and a little of the cooking liquid. Stir to make a paste.

Check the seasoning, add salt if desired, then when the chicken is nearly ready, add the saffron paste. Do not boil. Stir together when cooked and the sauce has thickened. Serve from a warm serving dish.

GARBANZOS AZAFRAN CON ESPINACA
CHICKPEAS WITH SAFFRON AND SPINACH

This recipe unites saffron and paprika, a happy and particularly Spanish combination. This is one of those recipes that can be extended with a little ham or chicken, or with other vegetables.

Serves 4 to 6

1 pound dried chickpeas, soaked
  overnight
1 pound potatoes, peeled
  and cut into chunks
2 hard-boiled eggs
¾ cup extra virgin olive oil
1 thick slice of French bread
1 clove of garlic, peeled and halved
1 onion, finely chopped

1 teaspoon paprika
30 saffron filaments, or ½ packet of
  powdered saffron, infused with 1
  tablespoon hot water
Salt
2 pounds fresh spinach,
  washed and chopped

Heat plenty of water in a large pot. When boiling, add the chickpeas, cover, and simmer. Add the potatoes and a little salt and cook for 30 minutes.
Chop the whites of the hard-boiled eggs. Reserve the yolks.
Heat some oil in a frying pan and fry the slice of bread. Remove then fry the garlic and remove. Slowly sauté the onion in the same pan, add the paprika and saffron infusion. Stir the contents of the pan in with the chickpeas.
Crush the garlic, bread, and egg yolk in a mortar and add to the chickpeas along with the chopped egg white.
Season with salt. Cook on a low heat for 15 minutes. Add the spinach. Finally, test the chickpeas to be sure they are cooked, then serve in soup bowls.

PERDIZ ESTOFADO
AUTUMN STEW OF PARTRIDGE

I first tasted this at the Parador Hotel in Albacete during the 1993 saffron harvest. I have also used quail, but other game birds may be well suited.

Serves 2 to 4

2 to 4 partridges, split in half
¼ cup olive oil
1 large onion, chopped
6 garlic cloves, peeled and crushed
2 bay leaves
6 peppercorns, crushed
1 cup dry white wine

1 carrot, sliced
8 small pearl onions, peeled
30 saffron filaments, or ½ packet of
    powdered saffron, infused in
    1 tablespoon white wine
Salt

Allow the partridges to sit, uncovered or lightly covered, in the refrigerator for 2 to 3 days. This helps to tenderize the meat and allow the flavor to develop. Heat the oil in a deep casserole, then brown the birds on all sides. Add the chopped onion, garlic, and bay leaves and cook until the onion is wilted. Add the peppercorns, wine, carrot, pearl onions, saffron infusion, and salt. Cover tightly and simmer about 1 hour, or until the partridges are tender. Parboiled, cubed, or whole new potatoes may also be added during the last 15 minutes of cooking.

RED PEPPER AND SAFFRON SAUCE OR SOUP

This is my favorite sauce for monkfish tails roasted with garlic and rosemary. With the addition of paprika, it is good with rabbit or lamb. If the sauce is kept thick, it becomes a dip for vegetables. It can also be diluted with stock to make a soup.

SAUCE

4 large red bell peppers
¼ cup extra virgin olive oil
1 red onion, chopped
1 garlic clove, minced
1 large vine-ripened tomato,
   chopped and deseeded

60 saffron filaments, or 1 packet
   powdered saffron, infused in
   1 tablespoon lemon juice
2 teaspoons chopped fresh thyme
Juice of ½ lemon
Dash of sherry vinegar
Salt and pepper

Brush the bell peppers with a coat of olive oil, then roast, grill, or barbecue until the skins are charred, blackened, and blistered on all sides. Remove the peppers from the heat and place in a heavy-weight plastic bag. Tie the bag with a knot and leave the peppers to steam for 15 minutes. This will make peeling them much easier. Heat the oil in a heavy pan and gently sweat the onion, then add the garlic and tomato, and cook for 20 minutes.

Peel the peppers over a bowl to retain all the juice and transfer any pepper juice in the bag to the bowl. Deseed the liquid by straining it through a sieve and reserve. Chop the pepper flesh and add to the onion mixture. Cook together for 2 minutes. Then add half the saffron infusion, the pepper juice, the thyme, the lemon juice, and the vinegar. Stir and simmer for 10 minutes, taste, and adjust the seasoning. Purée the mixture in a blender, then return it to the pan to warm to serving temperature. Stir in the remaining saffron infusion and serve.

SOUP

2 ½ cups vegetable or light chicken stock

Add the warm stock to the red bell pepper sauce. Cook for 5 minutes over low heat. Serve the soup garnished with a fine dice of raw red bell peppers, or a drizzle of extra virgin olive oil and sprinkling of flat-leaf parsley, or with a dollop of rouille or the Catalan Alioli.

PERSIA

"There is saffron and it is best in nature; it grows in several parts of Persia, but they esteem that above the rest which grows by the side of the Caspian Sea, and next to it is that of Hamadan."

SIR JOHN CHARDIN, *TRAVELS IN PERSIA*, 1673-1766

THE IMPORTANCE of Persian cuisine should not be underestimated; the world's first great civilization was sustained by the world's first great cuisine. The legacy of the elemental Persian kitchen can be enjoyed today, 7,000 years later, in the foods of both the East and the West. To know Persian cuisine is to understand the foundations of multinational culinary practice. The bequest of these ancient Persian cooks to us is good food, with many dishes flavored and colored with *za'farân*.

I am grateful to my publisher, Anne Dolamore, for giving me a copy of *The Legendary Cuisine of Persia* by Margaret Shaida. An inspiring read and a delight to cook from, Margaret's book is both fascinating and instructive. I further extend my gratitude to Margaret for allowing me to reproduce some of the excellent recipes from her book.

Suppliers of specialist Persian goods can be found in Appendix IV.

LIQUID SAFFRON

The Iranians usually grind the saffron pistils (filaments) to a fine powder and mix with warm water before adding them to their dishes. For easy reference, Margaret refers to this blend as "liquid saffron" in the recipes in this Persian section.

To make liquid saffron, ensure that the saffron is completely dry. If you suspect it may not be, put 20 to 30 pistils in a tiny mortar and place in a warm oven for a few minutes. Add half a dozen grains of sugar and with a pestle (or the back of a teaspoon) crush the saffron and sugar to a fine powder. If using within an hour or so, mix with 4 to 5 teaspoons of tepid water and leave to infuse to a deep orange color. If the ground saffron is mixed with boiling water it can be kept in a jar for several weeks.

PERSIAN-STYLE RICE

Since rice plays such an important and festive role in Persian cuisine, I feel I should relate a few old wives' tales (and a number of hints) about how and why the Persians first parboil and then steam their rice, and about how they serve and garnish it with saffron.

Serves 4 to 6

1 pound rice	1 tablespoon lemon juice (optional)
7 tablespoons salt	2 teaspoons liquid saffron
8 ¾ cups water	
6 tablespoons vegetable oil	**Garnish**
1 small egg	2 teaspoons liquid saffron
1 teaspoon yogurt (optional)	¼ cup butter, clarified

1. First, pick over the rice and remove any discolored bits or foreign matter. Wash clean in several changes of running water to remove all starch. This of course also removes much of the nutritional value, but in a country where rice is not the main source of nutrition and is consumed only occasionally, this seems relatively unimportant, given the resulting lightness of the end product.
2. To prevent the rice from breaking, set it to soak in fresh cold water mixed with ¼ cup cooking salt for each pound of rice. The water should stand at least 1 inch above the rice. Traditionally, chunks of rock salt were always used for this purpose. In Iran, where the rice is hard and the climate dry, the rice is soaked for many hours, usually overnight, but basmati does not require more than 3 hours. If it is soaked much longer, it will require less boiling and if soaked overnight, may quickly overcook and disintegrate.
3. Bring the 8 ¾ **cups** of water with 3 tablespoons of salt to a rapid boil.
4. The soaked rice should be drained and the excess water poured off (thus removing excess salt) and then poured into the fast-boiling well-salted

water. Stir the rice carefully so that all the grains are free-floating and bring back quickly to a boil. If the rice is not of the top quality, add the teaspoon of yogurt to the boiling rice to improve its appearance and taste. Some people use the water from strained yogurt to cook the rice in. If the rice looks liable to break, add a tablespoonful of lemon juice to prevent this happening.

5. After boiling for 2 minutes, the rice should be tested to see if it is ready. It is impossible to specify the exact length of time required to cook rice. It varies according to the fierceness of the heat, the thickness of the pan, and the amount of rice. A large amount requires almost no boiling time at all, because it tends to cook as the water comes back to a boil. It is best to test it frequently.

6. Scoop up a grain or two and test by pressing it between finger and thumb or by biting a grain between your teeth. It should be soft on the outside but still firm and slightly resistant in the center, but not hard or brittle. If not quite ready, try again in a moment or two. While waiting, resist the temptation to stir the rice: it serves no useful purpose (except in large saucepans over too small a source of heat) and can break the grains. When ready, strain immediately.

7. An ordinary vegetable colander is no good for straining because half the rice will disappear through the holes and down the sink. A mesh strainer is suitable provided it is free-standing so that the water can drain away immediately, but make sure it is large enough to prevent compression of the rice. The best and cheapest is a close-woven wicker fruit basket about 12 inches across. It can be placed over an ordinary colander so that the water just swishes away, and it is adequate for up to 2 pounds of rice. If you intend to cook very large amounts of rice frequently, it is advisable to invest in a free-standing rice colander, available in specialist kitchen equipment shops.

8. Rinse the rice thoroughly with tepid water. This is best done by rinsing out the saucepan and pouring the water over the rice.

9. Return the rinsed-out saucepan to the heat and pour in four parts oil to one part water, generously covering the bottom. While the oil and water are heating, toss the rice carefully several times in the colander to remove excess moisture and separate the grains as much as possible. When the oil is sizzling hot, take the rice up gently in a skimmer or slotted spoon and sprinkle into the pan. Continue to do this, building the rice up into a conicle shape. It is important throughout to sprinkle the rice. Never tip it all back in at once—this will squash and compress it. Make two or three holes in the rice by carefully poking the handle of a wooden spoon through it to the bottom of the pan. This releases the steam. Wrap the lid in a clean teacloth and put firmly on the saucepan so that no steam can escape. The teacloth absorbs the steam and prevents moisture from dripping back into the rice to make it soggy. Traditionally, some of the hot charcoals from the fire were heaped onto the concave lid of the pot to give an even heat to dry and cook the rice. More recently, a *damkoni*, a round closeknit raffia "lid" covered in several layers of cloth, is used for the steaming process, but a teacloth wrapped over the lid will do as well.

10. The rice should be left on a high heat for a few minutes until it is steaming. Iranian housewifes have a number of ways of ascertaining when the rice is steaming without actually removing the lid (which releases the steam and is thus ill-advised). Wet a finger and dab on the outside of the saucepan; if the wet patch sizzles and evaporates immediately, the rice is assumed to be steaming. But some experience with the same saucepan and burner soon leads to expertise. For those with less experience or confidence, a quick peek by lifting the lid slightly is sufficient to see if the steam is billowing. When it is, immediately lower the heat to medium-low for 30 more minutes (more for larger amounts), when the rice will be ready to serve. It can however be left on the very lowest heat of all for another hour or more without any deterioration, providing it is very gently steaming.

11. When ready to serve, put the hot saucepan on a cold, wet surface or in the sink with an inch of water in it. This releases one last burst of steam, and also makes the crispy bottom (*tahdeeg*) easier to remove.

12. Take up a skimmer of rice and mix carefully with the liquid saffron in a small bowl. Put to one side for garnish. Then, gently take up the rice with the skimmer and sprinkle it on to a warmed dish, building the rice up into a symmetrical mound.

13. Sprinkle the saffron rice over the top. Melt some clarified unsalted butter and pour through the skimmer all over the rice to give it a sheen.

14. Finally, remove the crispy bottom of the rice, preferably in one or two pieces, and serve on a separate plate.

The crusty bottom of the rice (*tahdeeg*) is considered a great delicacy in Iran, and is much sought after. It is rich, crisp, and tasty, and has a habit of disappearing in the kitchen before it ever reaches the table: the many helpers who always appear on the scene when the rice is being dished up exact a price for their assistance, which is often unwittingly paid with a crunchy piece of *tahdeeg*. However, the cook usually prevails to keep most of it intact. It's important that she should, because the golden *tahdeeg* is the ultimate proof of her ability to prepare perfect rice.

In some parts of the Middle East, the appearance of tahdeeg on the table is taken to mean that the bottom of the pot has been reached and the rice is finished. In Iran, it is too great a delicacy to deny to guests, and the entire pot will be turned out to get at it; everyone knows there is always lots more rice.

Tahdeeg results from putting the parboiled rice into the hot fat prior to steaming (at step 8 above). There are a number of ways to ensure a specially thick and rich *tahdeeg*:

• Beat an egg with a little yogurt and liquid saffron. Mix in a skimmer of parboiled rice and add to the sizzling oil, spreading across the bottom of the pan. Sprinkle the rest of the rice on top.
• Beat a small egg together with ½ teaspoon yogurt and 1 teaspoon tomato paste; mix in a skimmer of rice and pour into the hot oil.
• Lay thinly sliced rounds of potatoes in the hot oil.
• Lay a thin slice of Persian lavash bread (or pieces of filo pastry) across the bottom of the pan in the hot oil.

The saucepan (*deeg*) traditionally used for cooking rice in Persia is wide-based and slightly conical in shape, built to maximize the dying embers and to give a dry, even heat all round the steaming rice. It also has the advantage of producing large amounts of *tahdeeg*, delightfully out of proportion to the total amount of rice.

Suggested Saucepan Sizes

For easy reference, the following table gives relative saucepan sizes (with approximate conversions) for cooking rice:

For Plain Rice	For Mixed Rice	Saucepan Size
½ pound	125g (¼ pound)	2 quarts
¾ pound	250g (½ pound)	over 2 quarts
1 pound	350g (¾ pound)	nearly 10 cups
1½ pound	500g (1pound)	over 3 quarts
2 pounds	750g (1½ pounds)	nearly 14 cups
3¼ pounds	1kg (2 pounds)	15 cups
4½ pounds	1½kg (3¼ pounds)	over 1 gallon

MORASA' POLOW
JEWELLED RICE

In 1824 James Morier described this dish as "The King of Persian dishes," and there is little doubt that it raises the humble grain of rice to regal heights. Of all the festive dishes in Iran, this is the one chosen to be served at wedding banquets; it is thought to augur well for the young couple and to bring sweetness to their new life together. Yet despite its festive elegance, it consists of quite simple and easily available ingredients. It artistically blends the commonplace into pleasing harmony. At very extravagant weddings, the stunning dish with its golden saffron rice studded with gleaming "gems" (resembling diamonds, rubies, emeralds and topaz) is sometimes served in a swirl of spun sugar, which gives it a wonderful crunchy contrast to the soft textures and gentle flavors. It is an astonishingly beautiful and dramatic dish for special occasions and stands as shining testimony to the imaginative glory of Persian cooking.

Serves 4 to 6

1 pound basmati rice
6 tablespoons salt
2 pounds carrots
6 tablespoons vegetable oil
½ cup granulated sugar
6 teaspoons liquid saffron
½ cup plus 1 tablespoon water
Peel of 3 oranges

⅓ cup skinned almond slivers
⅓ cup skinned pistachio slivers
⅓ cup currants
1 teaspoon advieh spice mix
 (see page 101)
¼ cup unsalted butter, clarified
¼ cup crystallized sugar
½ teaspoon boiling water

Prepare the rice, using the salt, up to step 6 as given in the master recipe on page 95. Peel the carrots and julienne. Fry in oil over medium heat for 10 minutes, stirring constantly. Stir in a spoonful of sugar, 2 teaspoons of the liquid saffron, and 1 to 3 tablespoons of the water. Cover and cook for 4 to 5 minutes, or until the liquid is reduced. Put into a bowl and reserve.

Peel the oranges thinly (best done with a potato peeler to avoid pith) and julienne. Cover with cold water, bring to a boil, and strain. Repeat twice more to remove any bitterness. Reserve.

Brown 1 teaspoon of almonds in a frying pan and put aside for garnish. Put remaining almonds and all pistachios into a small saucepan. Cover with cold water, bring to a boil, strain, and reserve.

Bring the remaining granulated sugar and 6 tablespoons water slowly to a boil and simmer gently for 10 minutes. Add the orange peel and the nuts, reserving a teaspoon each of almonds and pistachios for garnish, and boil for 30 seconds. Strain and reserve the syrup. Put the peel and the nuts on one side.

Soak the currants in warm water for 10 minutes until plumped. Strain and reserve, reserving a teaspoon for the garnish.

At step 6, layer in the carrots, peel, nuts, and currants with the rice and sprinkle a little of the advieh over each layer. Finally, just before making the holes in the rice, pour over the remaining liquid saffron and syrup.

At step 10, garnish the rice with a sprinkling of toasted and untoasted almonds, the pistachios, and currants before pouring the clarified butter over all. Finally, chop the crystallized sugar, mix with the boiling water, and sprinkle over the rice.

SABZI POLOW
RICE WITH HERBS

This splendidly fragrant dish is the traditional meal of the spring festival, *No Rooz*. The first herbs of the new year are a feast for all the gastronomic senses: a delight to see, a treat to smell, and a joy to savor. The breath of spring is the aroma that fills the kitchen when fresh coriander, parsley, chives, and dill are being cleaned and chopped together.

The dark aromatic wedges of the herb omelette contrast perfectly with the delicate green and golden polow. In Iran, the first meal of the first day of the new year should include eggs (the symbol of birth), herbs (the symbol of growth), rice (the symbol of bounty), and fish (the symbol of freshness).

The flavor and fragrance of fresh herbs are the very essence of this dish, but the quantities required are not always available, especially in March when *No Rooz* is celebrated. It is at such times that dried herbs come into their own. Packets of dried herbs, weighing only 2 ounces yet sufficient to flavor just over 2 pounds of rice, are available at a number of Iranian foodstores in big cities. Some cooks take the best of both worlds, by using mostly dried herbs but adding a handful of fresh ones to give an added fragrance to the polow. The use of dried herbs, of course, does away with much of the work of cleaning, washing, and chopping.However, many Iranian housewives find the preparation of fresh herbs an occupation full of memories: in Persia, it means the house is filled with excited children, happy friends, and relatives gathering for the spring festival.

Serves 4 to 6

1 pound basmati long-grain rice	6 tablespoons vegetable oil
9 tablespoons salt	4 teaspoons liquid saffron
12 ounces combined fresh herbs (such as parsley, coriander, dill, and chives)	¼ cup unsalted butter, clarified
Tops of 2 garlic heads, or 1 dried garlic clove	2 sprigs fenugreek or ½ teaspoon dried (optional)

Prepare the rice, using the salt, up to step 6 as given in the master recipe on page 95.

Clean and wash the herbs, removing any coarse stems. Shake dry (or put in a salad spinner), chop finely, then spread out on several thicknesses of paper towel to dry. Cut the garlic leaves into 1-inch lengths and add to the herbs (the bulbs may be kept and dried). If using dried garlic, chop finely and add to the herbs.

When adding herbs to the rice at step 6, be sure they are free of excess moisture before layering them in with the rice.

Note: If fresh herbs are unavailable, use 1 ounce dried herbs, but add to the rice when it comes back to a boil. The rice and herbs will thus already be mixed when the rice is returned to the pan for steaming.

NORTHERN SAUCE

½ cup sugar
¾ cup lemon juice
¼ cup unsalted butter

2 teaspoons liquid saffron
Salt and black pepper

Gently heat the sugar with the lemon juice until dissolved, then add the butter to melt, the liquid saffron, salt, and pepper.

ADVIEH
SPICE MIX

This is an aromatic mixture to be used with special rice dishes. Grind together just enough for your needs as the fragrance will be lost over time. Reserve a little for a garnish, otherwise add the advieh for the last 10 minutes of cooking time.

20 saffron filaments, ground or
  ⅓ packet powdered saffron
⅔ cup shelled plain pistachios
1 ounce ground cinnamon stick

½ ounce green cardamom seeds
½ ounce dried rose petals
½ cup sugar (if making sweet or
  dessert rice)

TIKKEH KABÂB
CUBED LAMB KEBAB

Tikkeh means small piece. This is the classic lamb kebab so popular throughout the Middle East, Turkey, and Greece. The meat needs to be fresh and high quality, boned and trimmed. Marinate for 8 hours.

Lamb tenderloin is the prime cut for this dish, sliced, threaded on skewers, and alternated with slices of onion. Leg or shoulder cuts can also be used. It is best cooked on a medium heat on the grill. For Persian authenticity, the cooked meat should be sprinkled with *sumac*, the Persian table condiment available from Middle Eastern stores.

Serves 4
1 pound lean boned lamb
Marinade
2 medium onions
Juice of 2 lemons
Salt and pepper

Basting Sauce
¼ cup unsalted butter
Juice of 1 lemon
½ teaspoon liquid saffron

Trim the meat of all fat, cut into neat cubes, and wash.
Grate the onions into a bowl. Add the lemon juice, salt, pepper, and the drained meat. Mix well together, cover, and marinate for at least 8 hours.

While the charcoal is heating, prepare the basting sauce by mixing the melted butter, lemon juice, and liquid saffron (if using).

Thread the pieces of meat onto narrow skewers and grill over the charcoal, turning and basting until nicely browned and cooked through.

Serve with Persian (or pita) bread, fresh herbs, lemons, and sumac.

KHORESHT-E NÂRANJ
CHICKEN AND SOUR ORANGE STEW

The *naranj*, or sour orange, the Seville type, has been cultivated for over two thousand years in the Caspian region. The sweet orange named *portoghâl* was introduced by the Portuguese from China through the port of Hormoz.

Khoresht-e Nâranj should be made with sour oranges. Sweet oranges can be used in combination with lemon juice and a dash of vinegar, to simulate sourness.

Serves 4 to 6

1 large chicken (about 4 to 5 pounds)	3 tablespoons sugar or juice of 1 lemon
2 tablespoons olive oil	if using sweet oranges
2 medium onions	Salt and pepper
1 teaspoon ground cinnamon	**Garnish**
3 Seville oranges	1 teaspoon pistachio slivers
3 large carrots	2 teaspoons almond slices
½ teaspoon liquid saffron	

Cut up the chicken. Wash and pat dry. Fry in the oil until nicely browned. Remove with slotted spoon and put to one side.

Finely slice the onions and fry in same oil until soft and golden brown. Stir in the cinnamon. Add the chicken and enough water to cover. Put on lid and simmer gently for 30 minutes.

Peel the oranges (with a peeler) and julienne the peel. Put the zest in a small pan, cover with cold water, bring to a boil, and drain. Repeat twice more and leave to drain.

Peel the carrots and julienne. Fry in oil for 10 minutes then add to the stew with the orange zest. Simmer for 25 minutes.

With a sharp knife, remove the pith and skin from the orange segments.

A few minutes before serving, stir in the liquid saffron and the sugar (or lemon juice, if using sweet oranges) and add the orange segments.

Simmer for a minute or two and dish up into a warm bowl. Garnish with almond and pistachio slivers if desired and serve with plain white rice.

BOORÂNI-YE ESFENÂJ
YOGURT WITH SPINACH

The most popular of all the Persian *boorâni*, this dish can be found in many parts of the Middle East. It is traditionally served as a side dish in Persia, but it makes an unusual starter for a formal dinner, or a delicious light summer lunch. Serve with fresh Persian bread.

Serves 4

2 medium onions	¼ teaspoon turmeric
2 tablespoons olive oil	Salt and freshly ground black pepper
2 pounds fresh spinach or 1 small	8 ounces strained yogurt
package frozen spinach	1 teaspoon liquid saffron (optional)

Slice the onions thinly and fry in oil until soft and dark golden.
Wash the spinach thoroughly, shake dry, and chop finely. Add to the onions with the turmeric, salt, and pepper. Cover and cook gently until the spinach is soft.
Mix the spinach and onions together until well blended. Leave in a strainer to drain and cool.
Mix into the strained yogurt. Garnish with liquid saffron and serve chilled.

KOOKOO-YE SABZI
HERB OMELETTE

This is the most famous, and the most popular, of all *kookoo* (omelettes). It is the delicious symbolic accompaniment to *Sabzi Polow* (saffron rice with herbs, see page 101) served at the Persian new year in March.

But the herb omelette's soft and tenderly green center, encased in a crisply cooked dark exterior, is far too good to confine to spring alone. Full of healthy goodness, fresh eggs and herbs are easily available most of the year. The omelette can also serve as a delicious hot summer luncheon or light supper dish. It makes a lovely cold picnic snack.

As with all herb dishes, the weights given are only approximate. The longer the herbs sit around in stores, the less they will weigh—and, it must be said, the less tasty they will be. Another way to calculate the amount needed for ten eggs is to fill a level two-pint bowl with more or less equal portions of chopped parsley, coriander, and spring onions, along with a finely chopped leaf or two of lettuce and a sprinkling of fenugreek. Alternatively, one packet of dried herbs left to soak overnight may be used.

Some housewives add a tablespoon of chopped walnuts mixed in with the prepared herbs, but these additions are usually only for special occasions.

In Iran, the omelette is cooked in a frying pan and cut into eight segments which are carefully turned over individually. Alternatively, the omelette can be baked in a preheated oven at 375°. Place in bottom half of oven for 20 to 30 minutes. When omelette is firm to the touch, move to top half of oven for 10 more minutes. Cut into wedges and serve immediately. However, if using dried herbs, do not make the omelette in the oven or it becomes too dehydrated.

Cut into small squares and garnish with finely chopped walnuts. This makes an unusual cocktail snack.

1 bunch parsley	Salt and pepper
1 bunch cilantro	2 teaspoons chopped walnuts
1 bunch large green onions	(optional)
3 to 4 sprigs fenugreek,	10 medium eggs
or ½ teaspoon dried	½ teaspoon liquid saffron
1 to 2 lettuce leaves	
2 teaspoons all-purpose flour	
1 teaspoon baking powder	

Remove the coarse stems from the herbs, wash, shake dry, and chop finely along with the lettuce leaves. Pat dry , then put in a bowl.

Add the flour, baking powder, salt, and pepper. Stir the chopped walnuts into the flour mixture.

Break the eggs into another large bowl and whisk thoroughly. Add the saffron. Heat oil to cover a large frying pan, and at the same time, beat the herbs into the eggs. While beating, pour into the hot (not smoking) oil. Immediately reduce heat, cover and cook gently for 25 minutes, or until well risen.

Turn the omelette over and cook gently without a lid for 10 to 15 more minutes. When cooked through, remove immediately from the pan (to prevent unnecessary absorption of fat). Serve immediately, or leave to cool for a light snack.

SHOLLEHZARD
SAFFRON RICE PUDDING

A Persian rice pudding served with fresh fruits, tea, pastries and sweetmeats.

Serves 4

4 ounces pudding rice	2 tablespoons vegetable shortening
About 2 quarts water	Ground cinnamon
½ cup sugar	Almond and pistachio slivers
3 tablespoons rose water	
1 teaspoon liquid saffron	

Pick over, wash, and put the rice to boil in the water in a large saucepan over medium heat until very soft, adding more water as required and stirring from time to time, (Be careful it doesn't boil over.)

Stir in the sugar, rose water, and saffron and simmer until sugar is dissolved.

Reduce heat, melt the shortening, and stir in. Cover and simmer for 3 minutes.

Dish up into a serving bowl. When set, dust with the cinnamon and, if desired, sprinkle with almond and pistachio slivers.

HALVA
HALVAH

Halvah was originally made in pre-Islamic Persia as a celebratory dish. Known as *sen*, it was a fudge made of sprouting wheat, dates, walnuts, fennel seeds, turmeric, and oil. It was prepared on the last day of the new year festival to sustain the ancestors on their heavenward journey, following their annual visit to earth.

The conquest of Islam in the seventh century crushed many of the ways of the ancient religion, but it was less easy to alter people's eating habits. They continued to make *sen* (and still do in the southeastern Iran), but gradually another form of this fudge came to be made on the departure of loved ones to heaven. Today it is called *halva*, the Arabic derivative of "sweet," and it is a plain sweet dish made only on the occasion of the death of a close relative to be offered to mourners at the memorial service.

Other, more festive, and sweeter versions of halvah have come down to us. Quite different from this fudgelike sweet of ancient Iran, they are made of the precious sesame seed, plain or flavored with pistachios, and are popular all over the Middle East. They can be purchased ready-made at any Greek or Middle Eastern store.

1 cup sugar	4 teaspoons liquid saffron
½ cup water	½ cup unsalted butter
2 tablespoons rose water	1 ½ cups all-purpose flour

Boil the sugar and water together until the sugar is dissolved, then add the rose water and saffron. Remove from heat but keep warm.

Melt butter in a pan and gradually stir in the flour to a smooth paste. Cook over a low heat until golden in color.

Over a very low heat, slowly add the syrup to blend into a smooth paste. Remove from heat immediately.

While still warm, spread onto a plate and press down with the back of a spoon. Serve cold and cut into small wedges, accompanied by toast and tea.

IRANIAN SAFFRON CAKE WITH OLIVE OIL

This recipe is from Emily Green's column in the *Independent*. The original is by Richard de Cordova.

⅔ cup dried Iranian or Turkish
  morello sour cherries
¾ cup white cake flour
2 teaspoons baking powder
¾ cup whole-wheat cake flour
½ cup raisins
½ cup toasted almonds, cooled
4 eggs
1 cup plus 2 teaspoons superfine sugar

1 cup plus 2 tablespoons pungent
  green extra virgin olive oil
Grated zest and juice of 1 lemon
45 to 50 saffron filaments, or 1 packet
  powdered saffron infused in 1 tablespoon hot milk
3 tablespoons sesame seeds
2 tablespoons honey
  (preferably thyme honey)
Greek-style yogurt

Preheat oven to 350°.

Grease and flour a 10-inch cake pan, shaking out the excess. Just cover sour red cherries with boiling water in a small bowl. Sift together the white flour and baking powder. Sift again with whole-wheat flour, returning bran from sifter and mixing it in well. Mix raisins and almonds with 1 to 2 tablespoons of the flour mixture, or enough to coat them. (This will prevent them sinking in the cake batter.) Whisk together the eggs and sugar until smooth and thick. Gradually add small quantities of olive oil and flour until you have used all the oil and about half the flour. Add the lemon zest and juice, mixing thoroughly. Add the saffron infusion. Drain cherries, reserving liquid—you should have about ¼ cup of juice. Add 1 tablespoon of the remaining flour, followed by cherries, raisins, and almonds. Fold in thoroughly. Add remaining flour. Using a rubber spatula, transfer the batter to the prepared pan and sprinkle surface with the sesame seeds. Bake in the lower third of the oven for 35 minutes, or until a skewer inserted in the cake comes out clean. Resist opening the oven for the first 30 minutes.

While the cake is cooking, combine the cherry juice and honey in a saucepan and heat gently. When the cake comes out of the oven, allow to cool 10 minutes, then remove from the pan and immediately pour the cherry juice mixture over the top. Serve with a dollop of the yogurt.

INDIA

THE MAJORITY of recipes in this Indian section are from the Mughlai culinary tradition, the classical cuisine of India. This is the cuisine of the Maharajas, lavish and sumptuous. Many of these dishes and the cooking methods are of Persian origin, as a result of various conquests of India by both the Persians and Mongols. Etymology provides various clues: *biryani* is from the Persian *beryan*, which means "to bake." Nan, garam masala, pulao, and kabab are also of Persian origin. Therefore, it is no accident that the menus of many Indian restaurants in the States still feature a "Persian" section.

It was the Persians who introduced saffron into India, first its use as a spice and colorant, followed by its cultivation in Kashmir by at least 500 B.C.

The following recipes are authentic Indian recipes. I have compiled them with the help of many friends, who have provided me with genuine Indian cookbooks and some of their personal favorites. I am particularly grateful to Mrs. Rajeswari Mahalinghan of New Dehli for her contribution, and for the information she has given me regarding the culture and history of saffron in India.

I have reduced the quantity of chile by half in most of the recipes and I also omitted using the chile seeds, because for many the recipes would be too hot.

I recommend that you use real ghee for these Indian recipes, as it is the authentic fat for preparing Indian food with a definitive flavor which butter or cooking oil do not possess. Ghee is prepared from buffalo milk or vegetable sources and is available from specialty Indian stores.

ALMOND CHUTNEY

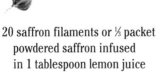

20 saffron filaments or ⅓ packet
  powdered saffron infused
  in 1 tablespoon lemon juice
⅔ cup almonds, blanched and chopped
2 to 3 roasted chiles, deseeded
⅔ cup fresh ginger, peeled and chopped

1 teaspoon cumin seeds, toasted
  or dry-fried and crushed
Rock salt
Chile powder to taste

Combine all the ingredients except the salt and chile powder in a food processor or mortar, working them into paste. Taste and adjust the seasoning of salt and chile powder. Allow some time for flavors to combine and develop before serving.

PLUM CHUTNEY

20 saffron filaments or ⅓ packet
  powdered saffron infused in
  1 tablespoon lime juice
½ cup dried plums
½ cup raisins

1 tablespoon cumin seeds, dry-fried
  and powdered
1 tablespoon chile powder
Juice of a large fresh lime
⅓ cup sliced almonds

Soak the plums and raisins in water for 20 minutes. Drain, then process in a blender with the cumin and chile powder until a thick purée forms. Add the lime juice and saffron and blend to combine all the ingredients. Allow time for the flavors to develop, then garnish with the sliced almonds. A little of the soaking water may also be added to achieve the desired consistency.

SWEET CHUTNEY

1 tamarind
1 cup hot water
20 dates, soaked in 1 cup hot water
  and drained
⅓ cup raisins, soaked in ½ cup water
  and drained
⅓ cup almonds, chopped
1 teaspoon garam masala
1 teaspoon ground ginger

1 teaspoon cumin seeds, toasted or
  dry-fried and finely ground
⅓ cup pistachios, sliced or shaved
Rock salt
Chile powder to taste
30 saffron filaments or ½ packet of
  powdered saffron infused in
  1 tablespoon lime juice

Soak the tamarind in the hot water for 20 minutes, then squeeze out the fruit's pulp and reserve.

Remove the seeds from the dates, then blend into a purée with the raisins and almonds. A little of the soaking water can be added to help the texture. (I prefer to use a little lime juice.)

Gently heat the tamarind pulp, adding the garam masala, ginger, and cumin. Then add the date-raisin purée, stir well, and taste. Adjust the seasoning with salt and chile powder; add the saffron infusion. Remove from the heat and allow to cool until the flavors combine. Garnish with pistachios.

GARAM MASALA

Garam masala is now widely available in prepackaged form from many of the major spice companies. However, the more dedicated of you may prefer to make your own. I like to make up large batches and pack it in light-proof, clay pots and give them to friends at Christmas. You will need to have the services of a first-class spice merchant to provide you with whole spices that you can grind yourself. Various kinds of spice mills and graters are available. The term garam masala is derived from the ancient Persian, *garm,* meaning hot, and *masaleh,* meaning ingredients.

⅛ ounce powdered saffron
¼ ounce black cumin seeds,
  dry-fried and finely ground
¼ ounce whole cloves, ground
¼ ounce bay leaves, finely ground
¼ ounce green cardamom
  seeds, finely ground

¼ ounce whole cinnamon sticks, ground
¼ ounce whole black peppercorns,
  ground
⅛ ounce mace, ground
⅛ ounce ground ginger

Combine all the spices and mix well. Store in a lightproof vessel away from any source of moisture. Use within six months.

NAVRATAN KORMA

Serves 4 to 6

50 saffron filaments, or 1 packet
  powdered saffron, infused in
  3 tablespoons hot milk
8 ounces cauliflower florets
4 ounces fresh shelled peas
4 ounces potatoes, cubed
4 ounces shredded carrots
4 ounces green beans
4 ounces mild hard cheese, sliced
3 garlic cloves, sliced and crushed
2 ounces fresh ginger, peeled
  and finely sliced
1 cup fresh cilantro leaves
2 green chiles, seeded
  and finely chopped
7 tablespoons ghee or oil

1 ½ tablespoons milk
1 teaspoon garam masala
1 teaspoon cumin seeds,
  dry-fried and ground
½ teaspoon turmeric
Salt
Chile powder
2 medium tomatoes, peeled, seeded,
  and puréed
8 ounces curd, beaten
2 tablespoons almonds
2 tablespoons cashew nuts, fried
Fresh fruits (such as pineapples,
  mangoes, oranges, and cherries)

Parboil all the vegetables. Refresh in ice water and set aside. Gently fry the sliced cheese in a nonstick pan and set aside.

Grind the garlic, ginger, cilantro, and green chiles into a paste then gently fry it in ghee or oil. Stir in a little of the milk, until it takes a golden color. Add all the vegetables and continue to cook on a low to medium heat. When the vegetables take on some color, about 5 minutes, add the garam masala, cumin, and turmeric. Taste, then adjust the seasoning of salt and chile powder.

Mix together, cook for 2 to 3 minutes, then add the tomatoes and cook, still over low heat, for another 2 to 3 minutes, then add the yogurt. Mix again and cook until the vegetables are crisp-tender. Mix in the cheese and the nuts and cook 1 to 2 more minutes.

Remove from heat and place on a serving dish. Sprinkle the saffron infusion over the top, garnish with the fruits, and serve.

ALMOND AND PEA CURRY

Serves 4 to 6

½ fresh coconut
2 cups boiling water
⅔ cup almonds
Oil or ghee for shallow frying
1 ounce fresh ginger, peeled
  and finely chopped
10 ounces fresh peas, shelled
  and blanched
½ teaspoon garam masala

½ teaspoon cumin seeds,
  dry-fried and ground
Salt to taste
1 tablespoon milk
50 saffron filaments or 1 packet
  powdered saffron infused in
  1 tablespoon hot milk
12 fresh mint leaves, chopped

Drain the milk from the coconut and reserve. Remove the white coconut meat from the shell, grind, and crush it to squeeze out the milk and reserve. Pour boiling water over the coconut pulp and leave to soak for 1 hour. Then squeeze the pulp dry and reserve the liquid.

Blanch a quarter of the almonds, then lightly fry them in a minimum of oil. When golden, remove, drain, and slice. Blanch the remaining almonds then grind them into a paste with the ginger.

Heat the oil or ghee and gently fry the almond paste to a light golden color. Add the peas, garam masala, cumin, and some salt. Stir all the ingredients together and add the coconut liquid. Over low-medium heat, cook until peas are soft, then add the coconut milk, simmer, and stir. Taste and add more salt if required. Transfer to a serving dish and pour over the saffron infusion. Garnish with the fried sliced almonds and mint leaves.

DUM ALU

Serves 4

10 almonds blanched	½ teaspoon mace
10 cashew nuts	Fresh thick curd mixed with
1 teaspoon poppy seeds	1 cup water
1 ounce fresh ginger, peeled	Salt
and chopped	Chile powder to taste
4 green chiles	3 tablespoons cream
1 cup fresh cilantro leaves	50 saffron filaments, or 1 packet
1 pound potatoes	powdered saffron, infused in
Oil or ghee, for shallow frying	1 tablespoon hot milk
1 teaspoon garam masala	2 slices fresh pineapple, diced
1 teaspoon ground coriander	3½ ounces fresh sweet mango, cubed
1 teaspoons cumin seeds	12 seedless grapes, sliced
½ teaspoon nutmeg	

Combine the nuts, poppy seeds, ginger, chiles, and cilantro in a blender and process to form a thick paste.

Parboil the potatoes, drain, and freshen under cold water. Cube the potatoes then prick the surface with a needle or fork. Deep-fry them in oil or ghee until golden, then drain and dry on a kitchen towel. In the same pan, fry the nut paste, garam masala, coriander, cumin, nutmeg, and mace.

Add the curd and water and cook over a low heat until the gravy begins to darken. Taste, and adjust the seasoning with salt and chile powder. Add the potatoes and continue to cook, increasing the heat until the gravy begins to boil. Remove from the heat and allow to cool slightly before stirring in the cream. Arrange on a serving dish and drizzle the saffron infusion over the top, then garnish with the fruit and serve.

EGG CURRY

Serves 4 to 6

10 eggs
12 almonds, blanched
⅓ cup unsalted cashew nuts
2 green chiles, slit and deseeded
1 ounce fresh ginger, peeled
  and chopped
1 teaspoon poppy seeds
¼ cup ghee
2 medium-sized tomatoes,
  blanched and sliced
3 tablespoons curd
1 teaspoon garam masala
1 teaspoon ground cumin

1 teaspoon coriander seeds
Salt
Chile powder to taste
1 cup coconut milk
50 saffron filaments or 1 packet
  powdered saffron infused in
  1 tablespoon hot milk
Garnish
10 pistachios, sliced
20 almonds, blanched, toasted,
  and sliced
Fresh cilantro leaves

Boil the eggs for 10 to 12 minutes, cool under cold water, and set aside. Blend the blanched almonds, cashew nuts, green chiles, ginger, and poppy seeds into a paste in a blender, food processor, or mortar.

Heat the ghee on medium-low heat, add the paste, sprinkle with a little milk, and mix well. After 5 minutes, add the tomatoes and cook 2 to 3 minutes and stir; then add the curd and stir. Add the spices, stir, taste, and adjust the seasoning with salt and chile powder. Cook together for a few minutes then add the coconut milk. Stir and reduce heat, so the mixture simmers.

Peel the eggs and slice lengthwise. Lightly salt them and place on a serving dish. When the curry mixture has thickened a little, give one final stir and pour over the eggs. Sprinkle the saffron infusion all over and garnish with the pistachios, almonds, and cilantro leaves. Serve with poppadoms.

LAMB SHAHZADA

Serves 4 to 6

This Indian-style roast leg of lamb is a modern-day adaptation of an ancient mutton recipe. If you find or wish to try mutton, marinate it in the spices for a day with some lime juice. Cook at more moderate temperature for around 3 hours.

2 medium onions, chopped
1 ounce fresh ginger, peeled
   and chopped
2 tablespoons poppy seeds
17 ounces sour curd
3 tablespoons garam masala
1 tablespoon coriander seeds,
   dry-fried and finely ground
1 teaspoon cumin seeds,
   dry-fried and finely ground
Salt
Chile powder

½ cup unsalted butter
4½ pounds leg of lamb, knuckle end
80 crushed saffron filaments, or
   1½ packets powdered saffron,
   infused in 1 tablespoon hot milk
1 cup cream
⅔ cup almonds, blanched and finely
   ground
¼ cup almonds, blanched, toasted, and
   sliced

In a blender, combine the onions, ginger, and poppy seeds into a paste. Mix the paste into the curd in a large bowl. Stir in the garam masala, coriander, cumin, some salt, and chile powder. Mix well together, fry, and leave for a while to allow the flavors to develop. Melt the butter and mix into the paste. With a sharp knife, make deep cuts into the meat, some down to the bone. Put the meat into the bowl with the paste and work it into the cuts and all over the surface. Preheat the oven to just under maximum temperature and roast meat for 15 minutes, then reduce the oven temperature to slightly over half and roast for a further 1 hour, depending on the weight of the leg. Check the meat to see whether it is cooked to your liking and then rest in a covered dish for 10 minutes, before carving. Collect any meat juices for the gravy. Combine the saffron infusion, the cream, and ground almonds and stir into the gravy. Cook for a few minutes to combine all the flavors. Add some water if it is too thick.

Arrange sliced roasted lamb on a warm serving plate and pour the gravy on and around it. Garnish with the toasted almonds.

BAHADURSHAHI BIRYANI
CHICKEN BIRYANI

This is a classic biryani recipe of layered saffron rice with rich, aromatic chicken. For a variation you could try rabbit or goat.

Serves 4
Marinade
Try to prepare this the day before so the chicken can marinate overnight—but if time is short even 1 hour will still make a difference.

3 medium onions, chopped

3 garlic cloves, crushed and chopped

3 green chiles, split, deseeded and chopped

1 ounce fresh ginger, peeled and chopped

4 bay leaves, crushed

2 tablespoons coriander leaves

2 tablespoons mint leaves

1 teaspoon garam masala

2 cinnamon sticks, crushed

15 ounces curd

½ teaspoon salt

Combine all ingredients in a blender or food processor, then marinate the chicken in the paste.

1 pound chicken pieces

1 cup plus 2 tablespoons oil

1 pound basmati rice

4 cloves

4 green cardamom, pods only

2½ cups hot water

½ teaspoon salt

80 saffron filaments, crushed, or 1½ packets powdered saffron, infused in 2 tablespoons of hot milk

Garnish
2 teaspoons fried nuts, sliced

2 medium tomatoes, sliced

1 teaspoon cilantro leaves

Heat 9 tablespoons of the oil then fry the chicken pieces and the marinade paste over a medium heat until the chicken starts to brown. Reduce heat and simmer for 30 minutes or until the chicken is cooked.

Meanwhile, prepare the rice. Pick over, wash, then soak the rice for 30 minutes and drain well. Heat the remaining 9 tablespoons of oil and lightly fry the cloves and cardamom. Add the rice, fry 1 minute, then add the water and salt. Stir and bring to a boil for 5 minutes. Reduce heat and simmer until the rice is dry and tender. Add more water if you need to. When ready, mix in the saffron infusion.

In a heavy-bottomed pan with lid, spread a layer of rice, then a layer of chicken, then rice, then chicken; the top layer should be the thickest of the rice layers. Put on the lid and seal with a flour and water paste.

Bake in a preheated 250° oven for 15 minutes.

Break seal, remove lid, and slide over a large serving plate. Turn upside-down to release the layered biryani onto the plate. Garnish with the nuts, tomatoes, and cilantro.

Serve with your favorite Indian bread and chutney.

BAHADURSHAHI FISH KOFTA CURRY

KOFTA

Serves 2 to 4

2 slices of white bread, crust removed
30 crushed saffron filaments, or
  1 packet powdered saffron, infused
  in 1 ¼ cups warm milk for 30 minutes
9 ounces fresh fish fillets or steaks
  (such as cod or haddock) gently
  poached, flaked, and deboned
1 large potato, peeled and cubed and
  cooked until soft in minimal water
1 large onion, chopped
1 ounce fresh ginger, peeled
  and chopped

2 cupfuls fresh coriander leaves,
  finely chopped
2 sprigs of mint leaves, chopped
¼ teaspoon cumin seeds, dry-fried
  and crushed
Salt
Chile powder
8 almonds, fried whole
Oil or ghee, for deep-frying

Soak the bread in the saffron-milk infusion for 20 minutes. Remove bread, squeeze out excess liquid, and reserve both. Mash the fish flakes with the back of a fork, mix in the potato, and then the saffroned bread. Combine all the other ingredients except the almonds and oil or ghee in a bowl, then add the fish mixture a little at a time mixing thoroughly together. Knead with your hands, then take one of the fried almonds and mold ⅛ of the mixture around it to form a kofta. Repeat until the entire mixture has been shaped. I make them in advance to allow an hour or two for the flavors to marry and develop, then I deep-fry them in medium-hot oil until lightly golden. Drain and hold in a warm serving dish.

CURRY

30 crushed saffron filaments, or
  ½ packet powdered saffron, infused
  in 1 tablespoon hot milk
1 large onion, chopped
1 ounce fresh ginger, peeled
  and chopped
2 garlic cloves, crushed and chopped
¼ cup ghee
½ cup fresh milk and the remaining
  saffron infusion from the bread

1 pound fresh tomatoes, blanched,
  peeled and chopped
1 teaspoon garam masala
1 teaspoon cumin seeds, dry-fried and
  finely ground
Salt
Chile powder
6 tablespoons fresh cream, lightly beaten
⅓ cup unsalted cashew nuts,
  lightly fried
½ cupful chopped fresh coriander

Prepare the saffron Blend the onion, ginger, and garlic into a paste then fry in the ghee. Sprinkle with a little of the milk. After 3 to 4 minutes add the tomatoes and cook for 5 to 8 minutes. Add garam masala and cumin. Stir well, taste, and adjust the seasoning with salt and chile powder. Cook for 5 minutes, increase the heat, and add 2 cups of hot water to bring to a boil. Reduce heat and gently simmer for 10 minutes.

Pour the curry over the Koftas and gently mix together. Then pour the cream around the edge of the dish in a continuous stream. Decorate the cream with splashes of saffron and, finally, garnish with the fried cashew nuts and cilantro leaves.

 # PRAWN PULLAO

This Pullao is strongly flavored with saffron, and the dish is finished in a sealed heavy ovenproof pot to "steam" the rice to perfection. I find a Spanish cazuela with a lid ideal for this method.

Serves 4 to 6

1 mug basmati rice	2 large cardamom pods
2 mugs water	½ ounce cinnamon sticks,
½ teaspoon salt	a full-size stick
2 eggs	1 large bay leaf
4 medium-sized onions, 2 cut into rings, 2 chopped	½ teaspoon nutmeg, freshly grated
2 ounces fresh ginger, peeled and finely chopped	½ teaspoon mace, pounded in a mortar
2 green chiles, split, seeded, and chopped	1 tablespoon cumin seeds, dry-fried and crushed
4 garlic cloves, crushed and sliced	1 teaspoon ground coriander powder
12 mint leaves	Salt
1 cupful fresh cilantro leaves	Chile powder
1 tablespoon poppy seeds	¼ cup ghee
8 ounces curd	80 saffron filaments, crushed, or
1 pound medium-sized prawns, cleaned, shelled, deveined, and halved lengthwise	1½ packets powdered saffron infused in ¼ cup hot milk
4 cloves	⅓ cup almonds
	⅓ cup pistachios blanched, fried and sliced
	⅓ cup raisins

Half-boil the rice in the water seasoned with the salt. Cook the eggs with the rice for about 10 minutes over a medium heat, and drain rice completely of water. Peel the eggs and put to one side. Fry the onion rings over high heat until brown, drain, and set aside.

In a blender, combine the chopped onion, ginger, chiles, garlic, mint, cilantro, and poppy seeds into a paste. Mix the curd into the paste, then add the prawns and the onion rings.

Briefly dry-fry or grill all the spices and incorporate into the prawn mixture. Let the mixture rest for one hour. Over low heat, cook the mixture for 20 minutes in a tightly covered pan.

Grease a heavy–bottomed ovenproof dish with a lid. Then arrange alternative layers of rice and the prawn mixture. Pour a little melted ghee and some of the saffron infusion over each layer. Start and finish with a layer of rice.

Pour more ghee over the rice and cover tightly. Seal the top of the pan with a stiff mixture of flour and water. Place in a 350° oven for 30 minutes. To serve, break seal and remove the lid. Slide a serving plate over the top of the rice then invert and lift the cooking vessel away from the plate. Garnish with the nuts, raisins, and sliced eggs.

KESARI CHAVAL
SAVORY SAFFRON RICE

Serves 4

8 ounces basmati rice
¼ cup ghee
1 inch-long cinnamon stick
3 whole cloves
2 large onions, finely sliced
2 ½ cups hot water

½ teaspoon salt
2 green cardamom pods
50 saffron filaments, crushed, or 1 packet powdered saffron, infused in 3 tablespoons of boiling water

Wash the rice and soak for 15 minutes, then drain thoroughly. Meanwhile, heat the ghee and gently fry the cinnamon and cloves, then increase heat to medium and fry the onions; do not brown. Stir, do not let it stick to the pan, and fry for 10 minutes. Lower the heat and fry the well-drained rice for 5 minutes. Stir the rice into the ghee so every grain is covered.

Add the hot water, salt, and cardamom pods and bring to a boil for 1 minute. Reduce the heat and stir in half the saffron infusion. Cover the pan and simmer the rice. Check for doneness after 20 minutes have elapsed.

When tender, stir in the remaining saffron infusion and serve from a warmed serving plate.

SWEET SAFFRON RICE

Serves 4 to 6

8 ounces basmati rice
¼ cup ghee
⅔ cup mixed almonds and pistachios, finely chopped
2 ½ cups coconut milk

50 saffron filaments, crushed, or 1 packet powdered saffron, infused in 2 tablespoons of hot milk
¼ teaspoon salt
3 tablespoons superfine sugar
Several drops rose water

Wash the rice and soak it for 15 minutes, then drain thoroughly. Heat the ghee over low to medium heat, then fry the nuts for 2 to 3 minutes. Add the well-drained rice and fry for 2 to 3 minutes more.

Add the coconut milk and bring to a boil, then reduce the heat and simmer. Add half the saffron infusion and salt. Stir. Add the sugar a little at a time, stirring so the rice can absorb the sugar before adding more. Cook until rice is tender and dry, around 20 minutes.

Stir in the remaining saffron infusion and a few drops of rose water, and serve.

 # SAFFRON SYRUP

This simple syrupcan be used with fruits, desserts, and pastry.

1½ cups water	40 saffron filaments, powdered and
2 cups caster sugar	infused in a little hot water

Put sugar and water into a saucepan and bring to a boil. Continue to boil for about 8 minutes, or until the mixture is reduced to one third of the original volume. Turn the heat down to very low and add saffron liquid. Leave to infuse. Serve hot or cold.

PEACH MURRABBA

Peaches preserved in a saffron-sugar syrup with nuts are delicious with sweet saffron rice (see page 119). You may wish to try this recipe with apples, cherries, or apricots.

Serves 6

60 saffron filaments, crushed, or
    1 packet powdered saffron, infused
    in 1 tablespoon hot water
⅓ cup almonds, blanched
⅓ cup pistachios

Oil, for shallow frying
12 ripe peaches
Juice of ½ a lemon or lime
½ cup sugar
2 cups water

Dry-fry the nuts for a few minutes. Remove from heat, cool, slice, then fry again in the minimum of oil. When the nuts start to darken, remove from heat. Dry on a kitchen towel and reserve.

Place the peaches in a large pan, cover with water, bring to a boil, and cook until the skin wrinkles. Plunge into a bowl of cold water to shock, then peel them. Cut the peaches in half and remove the pits. Pour over the lemon or lime juice over them to prevent discoloration, and reserve.

Place the sugar and water in a saucepan and bring to a boil. Then lower the heat and reduce the liquid. After 5 minutes, add the peaches and cook until they soften and the syrup thickens. Remove from the heat and cool. Stir in the saffron and then the nuts. Cool, then serve.

JALLEBI

Indian Jallebi are similar to doughnuts or churros: deep-fried dough sweetened with sugar. Serve at tea time or as a dessert, and have napkins and finger bowls handy.

DOUGH

30 saffron filaments, powdered, or	1 ounce dry active yeast
½ packet powdered saffron	5 ounces plain yogurt
¾ cup all-purpose flour	Cold water

SYRUP

30 crushed saffron filaments or	2 ⅔ cups granulated sugar
½ packet powdered saffron	2 ½ cups water
6 green cardamoms	2 ½ cups oil
6 whole cloves	Confectioners' sugar

Sift together the flour and powdered saffron, add the yeast, and mix in well. Mix in the yogurt. Add enough water to make a dough with the consistency of heavy cream. Cover with a damp kitchen towel and stand in a warm place for 4 hours to rise.

In a large heavy saucepan, briefly dry-fry the cardamom and cloves. Add the water and bring to a boil. Stir in half the sugar; when it has dissolved, add the remaining sugar and saffron. Continue to boil to evaporate the water until a heavy syrup forms. You need to reduce the mixture by two-thirds. Allow the mixture to cool.

Fill an icing bag fitted with a large-holed tip with the batter. Heat the oil to 360°. Then squeeze the batter into the oil, making a figure 8. Take great care with this process, as the oil can spit. Cook only one jallebi at a time. In hot oil, it will take around 1 minute for the jallebi to assume a light golden color. Remove from oil and drain, then immerse in the syrup for a few minutes. Repeat until all the batter is used.

Arrange the jallebi on a plate and dust with the confectioners' sugar. Any leftover syrup can be stored in the refrigerator for up to 1 week.

ITALY

THE ROMANS first embraced saffron as a spice, a medicine, and a dye. Aided by the spice merchants of Genoa and Venice during the Middle Ages, their legacy has endured to the present day. Saffron is cultivated in Italy, but so great is the passion for the most imperial spice that extra supplies are imported.

RISOTTO

Risotto has suffered a similar fate as saffron in England. Both have been misunderstood, shrouded in mystery, and adulterated. The commercially produced convenience risottos have further muddied the waters.

Risotto is originally a country dish, therefore the preparation and ingredients are ultimately of simple origin. Elaboration and variation have rightly occurred over many centuries, evolving into different styles regionally based; from Milan, Piedmont, Veneto, and Lombardy; and of the type of rice used in the dish.

Risotto (like paella) is principally a rice dish, therefore it is absolutely essential to use the correct type of Italian rice. Arborio is the most commonly recommended. It and Carnaroli are graded a "super-fino"; they are the starchiest and take the longest time to cook, 20 to 30 minutes. Vialone nano is graded as "semi-fino." It is the favorite of the Venice region, and will cook in about 15 minutes. The rice will release its starch to make a creamy thick sauce, while at the same time it absorbs the flavors of the stock and, in the case of Milanese, the color and flavor of the saffron. The rice will remain as individual grains, separate, nutty, and with some bite that is a little chewy. The final cooking of risotto takes place off the heat; it is the process known as *Mantecare*, the final swelling of the grains and the melting in of the butter and grated Parmesan cheese. I cover the saucepan during this process, as I find the gentle steaming of the rice helps the texture, though others may tell you not to.

The other vital ingredients for a successful risotto are good clear stock, a big, heavy steep-sided pan (not aluminium), and a wooden spoon, as the rice needs to be almost constantly stirred. The stock needs to be kept hot, just below boiling, and added by the ladleful; allow each to cook off before adding the next. Fry the onions and rice slowly on a low heat, then increase the heat just before you add the first ladleful of stock. Keep the heat constant for the duration of the cooking time. Add the seasoning near the end. If you should run out of stock before the rice is ready, add boiling water. Finally, risottos are always served on warmed plates or bowls.

 # RISOTTO ALLA MILANESE

I am grateful to Davie Eyre of The Eagle, London EC1 for showing me how to cook risotto and for giving me this recipe. David suggests serving this risotto with a meat course, such as osso bucco, oxtail, or grilled pork chops.

Serves 4

2 to 3 shallots or small onions,
  finely chopped
1 stick celery, chopped
2 ounces prosciutto fat or bacon or
  bone marrow, finely chopped
  (optional)
¼ cup unsalted butter
Olive oil

2 ½ cups arborio rice
4 ½ cups homemade light chicken or
  meat stock, warm
30 saffron filaments, or ½ packet
  powdered saffron, infused in
  a glass of white wine
Grated Parmesan cheese

In a heavy stockpot, gently fry the shallots or onions, celery, and prosciutto in half the butter and a dash of olive oil. Add the rice and continue to fry for 5 to 10 minutes more over a moderate heat; stir well to coat the grains. Add the saffron-wine infusion, boil, then follow with a ladleful of the stock. Add just enough to cover the rice so the stock will be absorbed within 3 to 4 minutes. Adjust the heat so the mixture bubbles gently. Stir the mixture gently. Add 4 to 5 successive ladlesful of stock.

Within 15 to 20 minutes, the rice grains will release their starch and the mixture will take on a creaminess. The aim is to produce separate grains that are soft on the outside and al dente inside.(The Milanese style of risotto is slightly sticky and compact.)

Remove from the heat when the risotto is cooked, 20 to 25 minutes. Stir in the remaining butter in pieces along with a couple of spoonfuls of Parmesan cheese. Allow to rest for 2 to 3 minutes before serving in warm soup bowls.

RISOTTO DE ZAFFERANO
E FIORI DI ZUCCHINI

RISOTTO OF SAFFRON AND ZUCCHINI BLOSSOMS

Many thanks to Alastair Little for allowing me to reproduce this beautiful risotto recipe. He says that, "it is a rich and spectacularly pretty dish where the taste of the saffron shines through without dominating the freshness of the zucchini. You have to be careful with saffron; use too much and the taste will be closer to the smell of dry cleaning fluid than to expensive magic."

Serves 4

VEGETABLE STOCK

4 carrots
2 onions
2 sticks celery, peeled and cut into
    a fine dice

1 tablespoon olive oil
1 bay leaf
10 parsley stalks
1 Glass dry white wine

THE RICE

6 zucchini
½ cup unsalted butter
1 ½ cups arborio rice
7 ½ cups vegetable stock

16 saffron filaments or ½ packet
    powdered saffron infused in
    ½ cup hot water
Salt and pepper
Parmesan cheese

Make the stock by sweating the vegetables in the oil until they glisten. Let them take on a little color but don't let them brown. Add the bay leaf, parsley stalks, and white wine, then pour in the water and simmer for 1 hour. Pass through a sieve, reserving the vegetables but discarding the parsley stalks and bay leaf. Return the stock to the saucepan and keep over low heat, just below boiling. Trim the zucchini and dice. Put 6 tablespoons of butter into a heavy, high-sided saucepan and sweat the diced zucchini in it for 2 to 3 minutes. Add the rice, turning and stirring with a wooden spoon until all the grains are shiny and coated. Add a ladleful of hot stock and the saffron infusion and stir until it is incorporated. Continue stirring, adding the stock a ladleful at a time. You will hear the rice clicking against the sides. It is impossible to say precisely how much stock the rice will absorb, but when it is nearly cooked (taste after 15 minutes to gauge this), add the reserved vegetables and chopped zucchini blossoms and the butter. Cook until the blossoms collapse, the butter is absorbed, and the rice is al dente.

Remove from the heat, cover, and leave it to stand for 2 minutes. Serve in large, warmed bowls or soup plates. Pass grated Parmesan at the table or set out a piece of cheese and a grater for your guests to help themselves.

FRANCE

SAFFRON'S role in French cuisine has been defined in a number of traditional, regional recipes over many centuries. It is an integral ingredient of both the modest country kitchen and the grand, Michelin-starred restaurant.

The most famous dish is Bouillabaisse, the Mediterranean fish soup of Marseille, which has two less well-known neighbors, both infused with saffron. They are Provencal *Bouride*, and the *Boullinada* of the Roussillon, in Catalan France, close to the Spanish border. All three are said to be of great antiquity, most probably of Phoenician origin, from a time when the Mediterranean Sea teemed with fish. Great cauldrons were prepared on shore, enriched with saffron from trading ships.

On the Atlantic coast, a *Mouclade* is found; mussels are poached in a saffron-wine stock that is finished with cream. At Easter time in the Auvergne, a festive *Mourtayrol* will be the center of attention at a family lunch; chicken is combined with other meats and vegetables in a rich saffron soup; the soup is then served first, followed by the chicken.

In France, as elsewhere, saffron has recently been rediscovered; its role reinterpreted by a new breed of chef. Many of their modern saffron recipes are to be found in the *Saveurs du Safron* by Bois and Aucante, published in Paris in 1993.

BOUILLABAISSE

Thackeray composed a Ballad of Bouillabiasse: "Green herbs, red peppers, mussels, saffern, soles, onions, garlic, roach, and dace: All these you eat at Terres Tavern in that one dish of bouillabaisse."

I am pleased to use this recipe of Rowley Leigh, for I remember another occasion when he helped my education regarding fish. My intercom sounded one morning in September 1977; it was Rowley. He announced we were going out to lunch. He had returned and was going to teach me how to eat oysters. We left my flat and headed down the Charing Cross Road to Sheeky's, a famous old-fashioned fish restaurant with a stylish oyster bar. After several dozen (I was shown the difference between native and pacific oysters) and a couple of black velvets, we were led to the main dining room, where I was to taste eel, in a simple stew, and grilled turbot for the first time. I recall we were the last to leave Sheeky's that particular lunchtime.

"The problem with making a real bouillabaisse is that of the fish," says Rowley, "some of them are difficult to find outside of Marseille, such as rascasse and small rock fish for the stock. It is occasionally possible to buy them in London, if not a very good bouillabaisse-style or inspired soup can be made using other fish."

"Quantities are difficult to state but it would be foolish to prepare bouillabaisse for less than 8 people, so you will need a large pan. Serious bouillabaisse is achieved by making a soup with the fish heads and trimmings or, better still, tiny rock fish, before making the actual bouillabaisse. Bouillabaisse does not incidently mean "boil like hell," but bring to a boil and then simmer gently (*abaisser*), a rather different kettle of fish."

THE SOUP

4 onions, sliced
3 leeks, chopped
3 fennel heads, quartered
1 head of garlic, each clove
   separated, peeled and crushed
⅔ cup extra virgin olive oil
2 pounds fish parts
   (heads and trimmings)
6 sweet tomatoes, cut into eighths
Orange peel
Peppercorns

1 bay leaf
1 handful chopped parsley
Sea salt
1 bottle dry French white wine
7½ cups water
1 big pinch saffron, or 60 filaments,
   or 1 packet powdered saffron,
   infused in white wine

In a wide, deep pan gently fry the onions, leeks, fennel, and garlic in the olive oil. After they have sweated for 10 minutes, turn the heat up and add the fish bits. Quickly brown the fish parts, then add the tomatoes, cook for 1 minute, then add the remaining ingredients and boil vigorously for no longer than 20 minutes. Remove from heat, then pass through a mouli and then a fine sieve. Keep warm.

THE BOUILLABAISSE

1 eel steak
1 rascasse steak
1 weaver
1 gurnard
1 monkfish
40 saffron filaments, or 1 packet
   powdered saffron, infused in
   3 tablespoons white wine
1 wrasse steak

1 bass steak
1 John Dory steak
1 whiting steak
Dash of pastis
Squeeze of lemon juice
Toast (recipe follows)
Rouille (recipe follows)

This is the final step, so be sure to have made the toast and rouille before commencing on the bouillabaisse.

Place the first five fish steaks in a big, wide pan and cover with the hot soup. Bring to a boil for 30 seconds, then simmer; add half the saffron infusion. After about 6 minutes add the wrasse, bass, John Dory, and finally the whiting. Exact timing is impossible to prescribe but it is essential to cook the fish on the bone to help it remain firm and integral. When the fish is cooked, remove (this may be at different times) and place on a warm serving dish.

Taste the broth, season with pepper and salt if needed, and add the remaining saffron, pastis, and lemon juice. Increase the temperature to just under boiling, let cook for 30 seconds, then serve in large, warmed bowls.

THE TOAST

Olive oil
1 baguette, cut into ½-inch-wide slices

Garlic clove

Brush the slices with olive oil and toast under a preheated broiler. Rub the slices with the garlic clove. Keep warm.

THE ROUILLE

¼ cup soup base
½ red chile
2 garlic cloves peeled, crushed,
    and chopped
3 generous tablespoons baked potato

40 to 50 saffron filaments, or 1 packet
    powdered saffron, infused in
    3 tablespoons lemon juice
2 egg yolks
Extra virgin olive oil
Harissa

Put the soup base into a small pan and heat. Add the chile, garlic, potato, and half the saffron infusion. Reduce the mixture until it becomes very thick, but do not let it burn. Pound, sieve, or blend into a smooth purée, then add the egg yolks. Work them into the mixture. Place in a large bowl and start to beat in the olive oil, slowly at first. As the sauce starts to emulsify, add the oil more quickly; stop when you have a smooth glossy sauce. Spoon in the remaining saffron infusion and stir, then add a little harissa; this rouille should be piquant.

To eat, place a piece of fish on the toast, top with a little rouille and consume with the soup.

(For variations, see other rouille recipes on following pages.)

 # ROUILLE

There are many variations of this ancient Mediterranean condiment, now a native of the south of France.

The classic rouille is made in a large mortar with a heavy, broad pestle—standard equipment in the Mediterranean kitchen. Purists would argue this is the best method for making rouille, but it does take a long time, approximately half an hour. We can use blenders or food processors to speed the process up.

The deep orange coloration of many rouille sauces served in restaurants is due to the addition of tomato, usually purée, a relatively modern ingredient. The anchovy can be viewed as optional, but be sure they are not too salty for the rouille; it may be best to rinse with water before using.

ROUILLE TRADITIONAL
THE MORTAR AND PESTLE METHOD

6 garlic cloves, peeled, crushed,
and chopped
¼ teaspoon sea salt or more to taste
1 anchovy fillet (optional)
1 teaspoon Dijon mustard
40 to 50 saffron filaments, or 1 packet
powdered saffron, infused in
1 tablespoon lemon juice for 1 hour

1 egg yolk
Pepper
1⅓ cups fruity extra virgin olive oil

Pound the garlic and salt into a soft, glossy mush; it will take about 10 minutes to do this properly. Mix in the anchovy fillet, mustard, and half the saffron infusion (minus filaments). Beat in the egg yolk until you have a smooth paste.

Start to add the oil, slowly at first, beating all the time. As the sauce starts to form it will become lighter in color as more oil is incorporated. At this stage, beat with a whisk and add enough oil, drop by drop, until it emusifies. Spoon in the remaining saffron infusion, including the filaments. Allow the sauce to rest for 30 minutes before serving.

ROUILLE MODERN
THE FOOD PROCESSOR OR BLENDER METHOD

Rouille can be made completely in either machine in a matter of minutes. Or, you can combine all the ingredients except the oil in the machine, then transfer to a large bowl and beat in the oil by hand with a whisk. Use a smooth, fruity olive oil, preferably from the south of France, for best results.

40 to 50 saffron filaments, or 1 packet
   powdered saffron, infused in
   1 tablespoon lemon juice for 1 hour
2 garlic cloves, peeled and crushed
2 anchovy fillets
1 teaspoon tomato purée
1 teaspoon Dijon mustard
Pepper

1 teaspoon hot chile sauce
2 hard-boiled egg yolks
1 raw egg yolk
Extra virgin olive oil

Combine one-half to three quarters of the saffron infusion with all the other ingredients, except the raw egg and oil, in the food processor. Add the raw egg and beat until a smooth evenly mixed paste forms.

With the motor running at a slow beat, start to pour in the oil, slowly at first, so the mixture can absorb each addition before adding the next. The sauce will start to lighten in color as more oil is absorbed. Stop adding oil when the desired consistency is reached.

Transfer the mixture to a serving bowl, stir in with a spoon the remaining saffron infusion, and let rest for 15 minutes to allow the flavors to develop.

LES TRIPES AU SAFRAN À L'ALBIGEOISE

This tripe in saffron sauce is in the style of Albi, from *Goose Fat and Garlic*, by Jeanne Strang. The town of Albi is in southwestern France near Toulouse. It was a saffron-growing region for many centuries, and this is one of the town's most famous recipes.

Serves 4 to 6

2 ¼ pounds beef tripe
   1 pig's or calf's foot
   Piece of ham bone (optional)
2 onions, 1 stuck with 3 whole cloves
2 carrots
Bouquet garni

3 cloves garlic
¾ cup dry white wine
4 ½ cups stock
Salt and pepper

In Britain, tripe is usually sold already blanched. If not, you must plunge it in lightly salted boiling water for 5 minutes. This will give off a most disagreeable smell, which you must not allow to put you off the whole dish.

Cut the blanched tripe into 2-inch squares and put them in a pan with a tight-fitting lid that is large enough to hold the other ingredients and is good for slow simmering. Cover the vegetables and the other meats, packing them as tightly as reasonably possible—the more concentrated your bouillon in the end, the better. Add the wine and stock. Season lightly and slowly bring to a boil. Cover and simmer gently for at least 8 hours—the longer the better—over very low heat.

For the sauce
3 tablespoons goose fat
4 ounces salt belly of pork or
   unsmoked streaky bacon,
   finely diced
1 onion, finely chopped
2 cloves garlic, finely chopped
2 tablespoons chopped parsley

¼ cup flour
50 saffron filaments, or 1 packet
   powdered saffron, infused in
   1 tablespoon white wine
3 tablespoons capers, plus
1 rounded tablespoon caper juice
3 tablespoons armagnac

An hour or so before you intend to serve the dish, take a flameproof serving dish and in it melt the goose and pork fat. Add the onion, garlic, and parsley and soften all together slowly for 10 minutes. Stir in the flour and cook for 2 to 3 minutes. Ladle the tripe from the other pan into this roux and gradually moisten with enough of the tripe stock to bring the roux to the consistency of thin cream. Stir in the saffron infusion. Cover the pot and cook for 40 minutes. Just before serving, add the capers and their juice and the armagnac and check the seasoning. Steamed or boiled potatoes are a good accompaniment, with a crisp salad to follow. Whatever you do, do not spurn the extra stock. When it cools, it will turn into a marvelous transparent jelly, as deep in flavor as it is in color.

PUMPKIN WITH SAFFRON

This is a delicate and delicious recipe from the south west of France, taken from *Goose Fat and Garlic* by Jeanne Strang.

12 ounces pumpkin, peeled and
    deseeded
1 tablespoon goose fat or butter
1 tablespoon cornmeal

30 saffron filaments, or ½ packet
    powdered saffron, infused in
1 tablespoon of hot milk
¼ cup milk
Salt and pepper

Coarsely chop the pumpkin. Heat the fat or butter in a heavy-bottomed casserole or pan, and let the pumpkin sweat in it until it turns translucent and soft. This may take up to 30 minutes, depending on the age of the pumpkin. Do not let it fry; when soft enough, mash it with a wooden spoon in the pan until you have a coarse purée, then stir in the cornmeal and saffron infusion. Blend in the milk, season with salt and pepper, and let it all simmer together; stir for 5 minutes. You will find you have a beautiful gold-colored light purée with a delicate flavor.

SWEDEN

LUCIA

The celebration of St. Lucia's day on December 13 is a uniquely Swedish occasion: a festival of light to enjoy at the depth of their dark Nordic winter.

Festivities commence before the late lilac-gray dawn with a special breakfast of sculptured saffron buns, made from a wheat flour yeasted dough the color of sunlight (see page 136 for recipe). They are baked in many intricate shapes or braided forms, the most and popular being *lussekat*, "Lucia cats." They are feline shaped with currants for eyes. There are other regional shapes, including "Lucia's crown," "sheafs of wheat," "lilies," "hearts," "figures of eight," "wagons," "wild boar," and a "sword hilt in a scabbard."

Religious motifs from much earlier Christmas traditions are also used and include "apostle cake," "Priests' locks" (hair or wig shaped), beautifully molded "church doors," "a seven-hole twist," and Christmas star and cross shapes.

The twilight day continues with shimmering candle-lit processions of Lucia, headed by a local blonde girl robed in white with a red sash. She wears a halo-like crown on her head, made from a wreath of loganberry sprigs adorned with candles or, nowadays, battery-powered lights. Festive and religious songs are performed and Lucia hands out more saffron buns.

Lucia festivities are of German/Lutheran origin and date from when the Reformation had forbidden the adoration of the saints. Lucia is, in fact, a reinterpretation of St. Nicholas, the saint of children, and other Christmas traditions. There is a connection with the Sicilian St. Lucia; however her name is derived from the Latin word for light, *Lux*. The Lucia tradition began in the west of Sweden, then spread nationally during the latter part of the 19th century. The first Lucia parade in Stockholm was held in 1927. The Lucia tradition has traveled wherever Swedish people have, and thousands of saffron buns are baked in celebration each December by the Swedish Church in New York City and by other Swedish communities worldwide. Lucia festivities are also celebrated in London, at the Swedish Church near Baker Street, and at the Barbican Center.

SAFFRANSBULLAR
SWEDISH SAFFRON-BRAIDED
CHRISTMAS BREAD AND "LUCIA CATS"

Makes 12

2 packets active dry yeast
⅔ cups warm water (108°)
½ cup sugar
6 tablespoons butter,
   warmed to melting
1 cup cream
100 saffron filaments, dry-fried
   and powdered, or 2 packets
   powdered saffron

2 eggs, at room temperature
4 ½ cups unbleached plain flour

For the glaze
1 egg
3 tablespoons milk

In a large warm mixing bowl, dissolve the yeast in the warm water with 2½ teaspoons of the sugar. Briefly whisk together and leave until it foams, 5 to 10 minutes. Add the remaining sugar, the butter, cream, saffron, and eggs. Beat well. Stir in the flour, 1 cup at a time, beating well to keep the mixture smooth and satiny. Cover and refrigerate for 2 to 24 hours.

Cut the chilled dough into 3 pieces. On a lightly floured board, roll each piece into a rope about 1 yard long. Braid the 3 ropes of dough together and pinch ends together to seal. Place on a baking sheet covered with parchment paper or lightly greased.

Whisk the egg and milk together then brush on the braided loaf. Cover and place in a warm place to rise until doubled in size.

Preheat the oven to 375° and bake for about 30 minutes or until golden.

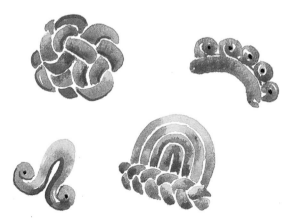

SAFFRANSKUBBAR
SWEDISH SAFFRON BUNS WITH ALMONDS

Makes 20 buns

100 saffron filaments, dry-fried
   and powdered, or 2 packets
   powdered saffron
¾ cup flour
½ teaspoon salt
1 tablespoon sugar

12 almonds, finely chopped
½ cup butter or margarine
1 egg
⅔ cup milk
1 egg, beaten
Pearl sugar

Mix saffron, flour, salt, sugar, and almonds in a bowl. Add the butter, in small pieces, evenly into the mixture. Stir in the egg and milk. Work into a dough. Split the dough in half and roll out into two lengths. Divide each length into 10 pieces. Brush each bun with the beaten egg mixture and then sprinkle some pearl sugar over each bun.

Place the buns on a greased baking tray and bake in the middle of a preheated oven at 425° for 12 to 15 minutes.

SAFFRANSKAKA
SWEDISH SAFFRON AND ALMOND CAKE WITH APPLE

100 saffon filaments, dry fried and
  powdered, or 2 packets
  powdered saffron
3 egg yolks
¾ cup plain flour
1 teaspoon baking powder
9 ounces almond paste, chilled

½ cup plus 2 tablespoons
  butter, chopped
3 egg whites, stiffly beaten
2 apples peeled, cored, and
  thinly sliced
1 tablespoon sugar

In a large mixing bowl, combine the saffron powder and egg yolks and beat.
Start to add the flour, beating continuously and incorporating the flour before
adding more. Mix in the baking powder.

Roughly grate the almond paste and mix in. Add the butter and stir. Fold in the
egg whites.

Grease a round cake tin and pour in the mixture. Cover with one layer of apple
slices, lightly pressing them into the top, then adding another layer of apple
slices on top. Sprinkle the sugar over the apples and add a few small pieces of
butter.

Bake at 350° for about 45 minutes, remove from oven, and allow to cool before
turning out of the tin and slicing.

REST OF THE WORLD

SO MANY COUNTRIES and peoples share a culinary heritage; similar saffron recipes can be found in both East and West. Other than rice, the most common thread is the baking of saffron cakes and bread, especially to celebrate Easter. Many old, traditional recipes from Europe were brought to America by emigrants—Swedes, Cornish and the Pennsylvania Dutch (who were in fact Germans).

Conquest by invading armies, followed by a long period of occupation, has also influenced the cuisine of many nations. The Persians introduced saffron into India, and the Moors took it to Spain and Sicily, for example.

Here is a selection of recipes from around the world, some traditional, such as *Zerde* and *Kulich,* and others useful, modern, and delicious.

URBEKSKII PLOV
UZBEKISTAN-STYLE PILAF

This plov recipe is from the central Asian republic of Uzbekistan. Cooked in the open air, in vast cauldrons over a wood fire, it is often available from street vendors on market day in the ancient city of Bukhara.

Serves 6

2 pounds boneless lamb shoulder
   or leg with some fat
3 tablespoons olive oil
2 large onions, chopped
3 carrots, julienned
13 ounces basmati rice,
   washed and soaked
4 ½ cups boiling water
1 teaspoon chopped red chile

1 teaspoon salt
1 teaspoon black pepper
60 saffron filaments, or 1 packet
   powdered saffron, infused in
   1 tablespoon hot water

Garnish
Sweet onions, sliced paper thin

Cut the lamb into chunks. Heat the oil in a sauté pan. Add the lamb and brown, then remove and keep warm. In the same oil, fry the chopped onions and carrots over a low heat until tender but not brown.

Add the rice to fry (add more oil if needed), stir the rice, and continue to cook for about 5 minutes. Return the lamb to the pan, mix into the rice, then add the boiling water.

Add the chile, salt, pepper, and half the saffron infusion. Cover and cook over low heat until the rice is tender, about 20 minutes. Stir in the remaining saffron infusion and garnish with the slices of raw onion.

KULICH
A RUSSIAN EASTER SAFFRON BREAD

The baking of special saffron breads and cakes to commemorate religious or festive occasions is widespread.

Paskha, the Easter celebrations of the Russian Orthodox Church would not be complete without a kulich, a tall, cylindrical saffron loaf with a billowing, mushroom-shaped crown. It is traditionally served with a *paskha*, a rich pyramid-shaped cheese cake, and the spectacular painted Easter eggs known as *pisanki*.

Kulich recipes are treasured and passed on by each generation; many still in use are centuries old. Kulich is baked in a tall mold (up to 12 inches high). It will probably be necessary to improvise a vessel for this purpose. A large coffee can could be substituted. However, be prepared to cut the bottom out to aid removal of the loaf from the tin. In Russia it is traditional to turn out the kulich on a large, thick down pillow. It is then carefully rolled from side to side to cool; the pillow allows the kulich to retain its shape.

On Easter, the crown is removed and the loaf is sliced horizontally; then the crown is then replaced to retain freshness and the kulich's visual appeal.

1 packet dry active yeast
6 tablespoons lukewarm water
¾ cup sugar
½ cup warmed milk
4 cups plus 5 tablespoons flour
½ cup unsalted butter,
   at room temperature
8 egg yolks
1 vanilla pod, pulp scraped out
60 saffron filaments, crumbled, or
   1 packet powdered saffron, infused
   in 1 tablespoon dark rum

¼ cup candied orange peel
3 tablespoons currants
¼ cup sliced blanched almonds
2 egg whites, beaten
¼ teaspoon salt
Icing
confectioners' sugar
½ teaspoon almond extract
3 to 4 tablespoons hot water

Dissolve the yeast in the lukewarm water. Stir in the ½ cup of sugar and the warmed milk, then add 9 tablespoons of the flour. Mix together, cover, and then leave to rise for about 1 hour.

Cream together the butter and remaining ¼ cup of sugar, then beat in the egg yolks. Add in the proofed yeast and the vanilla pulp. Stir in the saffron-rum infusion and salt. Add enough of the remaining flour to make soft dough, then mix in the orange peel, currants, and nuts.

Carefully fold the beaten egg whites into the dough. Turn the dough out onto a lightly floured board and knead gently until elastic. Place the dough into a greased bowl. Turn it in the bowl to coat lightly with grease. Cover and leave to rise, in a warm place, until doubled in size, up to 2 hours.

Grease your chosen mold and then line it with greased parchment paper, turning the top edge over the top of the mold to support the crown.

Punch down the dough, then knead lightly, and place in the mold. Only fill the mold about two-thirds. Leave it to rise until the dough reaches the top of the mold. Meanwhile preheat the oven to 400°and bake the kulich for 10 minutes. Then reduce the heat to 350° and continue to bake for 35 to 40 more minutes. While the loaf is baking, prepare the icing. Sift the confectioners' sugar, then stir in the almond extract and enough of the hot water to make a pourable icing that is not too thin.

When baked, turn out the kulich and glaze with the icing while still warm. kulich is often taken to church to be blessed and decorated with fruit, nuts, and a single white candle or gold crosses.

BABA SZAFRONOWA
POLAND'S TRADITIONAL EASTER CAKE

Szafronowa is another variation of the sweet, yeasted, saffron-flavored dough cakes found elsewhere.

Baked specifically at Easter, this cake has the added flavor of lemon peel that has been steeped in pure Polish spirits for 3 hours before it is combined into the dough. I thank Chris Polazek for introducing me to this very precious Polish tradition.

MUSSELS IN A CREAM SAFFRON SAUCE WITH NOODLES

Günther Schlender claimed this was his favorite dish for over 20 years when it was featured in an article in the *Caterer and Hotelkeeper* in 1989. His *moules á la crème de safran aux nouilles verts*, was prepared with some homemade noodles.

Serves 4

40 large mussels
¾ cup unsalted butter
1 generous tablespoon chopped onion
1 generous tablespoon chopped parsley
½ bottle dry white wine
Sauce
¼ cup butter
2 shallots, diced
1 scant tablespoon tomato purée

40 to 50 saffron filaments, or 1 packet
   powdered saffron, infused in
   3 tablespoons white wine
¾ cup heavy cream
Salt and pepper
Juice of 1 lemon
1 pound dried linguine or other
   noodles, cooked al dente
Garnish
Finely diced chives or parsley

Scrub and debeard the mussels. In a heavy pan, melt ¾ cup of the butter, add onion, parsley, and half the wine. Bring to a boil and add mussels and cook, shaking the pan periodically until the mussels open. Discard any that do not open. Remove each from the pan with a slotted spoon; ensure that all of the mussels' juices remain in the pan. Reduce the contents of the pan for 2 minutes, strain this mussel stock, and reserve.

SAUCE

Sweat shallots in the ¼ cup of the butter for 5 minutes. Add tomato purée, half the saffron infusion, and the rest of the wine. Add reserved mussel stock reduction and reduce again by one-half to two-thirds of the original volume. Taste, remove from heat for a few minutes, and add the cream. Reduce again to thicken if needed, adding salt, pepper, and a little lemon juice to taste.

Bring the sauce to a simmer and stir in the remaining saffron infusion. Place mussels in sauce to warm. Pile pasta on each warmed soup plate. Divide the mussels among the plates, then divide the sauce among the plates. Garnish with finely diced chives or parsley.

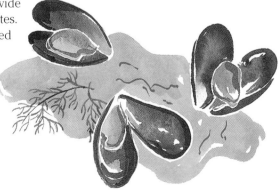

ZERDE "A MOUND OF GOLD STUDDED WITH RUBIES"
TURKISH RICE FLAVORED WITH SAFFRON AND POMEGRANATE

"Pomegranate, saffron, cinnamon, the ingredients of love," from the groom's speech in the Song of Solomon, are perfumed by rose water in this celebratory rice feast. No wedding in Anatolia is complete without a Zerde to this day. It is a truly romantic dish and is often served from a dome-shaped pilaf. I thank Nevin Halici for this recipe, which is from her *Turkish Cookbook*.

Serves 4

⅓ cup rice
1 cup water
¾ cup superfine sugar
40 saffron filaments, or ⅔ packet powdered saffron, infused overnight in 1 tablespoon rose water

1 teaspoon cornstarch
2 teaspoons warm water
¼ cup pinenuts, toasted
1 teaspoon ground cinnamon
Seeds of ½ pomegranate
¼ cup currants

Pick over and wash the rice if you need to. Cook the rice in the water over very low heat for 25 to 30 minutes, until tender. During the last 10 minutes of cooking add the sugar in 3 stages while stirring, allowing each addition to dissolve before adding the next.

Stir in the saffron–rose water infusion. Blend in the cornstarch with the warm water, then add, a little at a time, to the rice and stir. Cook for 5 minutes. Remove the rice from heat and place in a bowl to cool. Mix in half of the pinenuts, the cinnamon, pomegranate seeds, and currants. When cool, garnish with the pinenuts, cinnamon, pomegranate seeds, and currants and serve.

CHERMOULA

I found this spicy Moroccan seasoning, which is used as a marinade, then cooked with meat, chicken, or fish, in Michael Bateman's column in *The Independent on Sunday*.

60 saffron filaments, dry-fried and crumbled, or ½ packet powdered saffron infused in 1 tablespoon lemon juice
½ bunch fresh cilantro leaves, finely chopped
3 garlic cloves, crushed and chopped

2 teaspoons coarse salt
1 teaspoon ground cumin
1 teaspoon hot paprika
½ teaspoon ground cayenne pepper
9 tablespoons extra virgin olive oil
3 tablespoons lemon juice

Combine all the ingredients, and then use as a marinade. I use chermoula to marinate meat before grilling and as a basting sauce while the meat is cooking.

MOROCCAN 4-SPICE CHICKEN WITH LEMON AND OLIVES

I thank the late Jane Grigson for this recipe. I enjoyed a very similar dish in Tangier some years ago and had been searching for a recipe to replicate it. At first glance, it may seem a lot of work but it is well worth the trouble. You may wish to add a little harissa. The chicken carcass and any leftovers can be made into a delicious soup.

Serves 4 to 6

For the marinade

1 teaspoon ground ginger
½ teaspoon paprika
¼ teaspoon ground cumin
¼ teaspoon turmeric

2 garlic cloves, crushed
3 tablespoons olive oil
1 corn-fed or other quality chicken

For the chicken

2 lemons
½ cup green olives
1 large onion, very finely chopped
¼ cup packed parsley leaves
¼ cup packed chopped cilantro leaves

30 saffron filaments or ½ packet
   powdered saffron infused in
   a little lemon juice
Black pepper

Mix the ginger, paprika, cumin, turmeric, and garlic with the oil. Pour this mixture over the chicken and work it into all the crevices. Leave the chicken and spice mixture to marinate overnight. Peel and seed the lemons, cut in quarters, cover with salted water, and reserve. Split and pit the olives. Simmer in water; if the olives are very salty change the water several times.

Place the chicken in a deep pot and add the onion, parsley, cilantro, and half the saffron infusion. Half fill the pot with water. Bring to a boil, cover, reduce heat by half, and cook for 1 hour. Turn the chicken in the pot from time to time. Check the chicken as it cooks. You may need to increase temperature and/or the time. When nearly ready, reduce heat to very low, then add the lemons and olives. Stew together for 10 minutes.

Transfer the chicken, lemons, and olives to a hot serving dish and cover. Meanwhile, increase the heat and reduce the remaining cooking liquid by half. Taste the sauce, and add the remaining saffron and a generous amount of black pepper. Stir and cook 1 minute. Pour over the chicken and serve with rice or couscous.

EGGPLANT PANCAKES WITH SAFFRON SALMON AND ENDIVE

This recipe is from Michael Roberts's column published in the *San Francisco Examiner*.

Serves 4

1 medium eggplant
3 tablespoons olive oil
1 tablespoon finely minced garlic
2 tablespoons finely minced shallot
   or onion
7 tablespoons flour
½ teaspoon baking powder
2 eggs
9 tablespoons chicken stock or
   low-sodium chicken broth
3 tablespoons chopped parsley
2 teaspoons salt
½ teaspoon freshly ground pepper

6 tablespoons unsalted butter
9 tablespoons dry white wine
9 tablespoons whipping cream
50 saffron filaments, or 1 packet
   powdered saffron
1 pound skinless salmon fillets,
   cut into 1-inch cubes
1 medium red bell pepper, diced into
   ¼-inch pieces
12 to 16 Belgian endive spears

Bake eggplant on baking sheet at 350° for 30 to 35 minutes, turning every 10 minutes. When the flesh is very soft and wrinkled, remove from oven. Cut eggplant in half and scoop flesh into mixing bowl. Mash with fork until smooth. Heat olive oil in small saucepan. Add garlic and shallot, and sauté over low heat for 1 minute. Mix in eggplant purée along with ⅓ cup of flour and the baking powder. Stir in eggs, stock, parsley, 1 teaspoon of the salt, and the pepper.

Melt 1 tablespoon of the butter in a skillet over medium heat without letting it burn. Drop soup spoonfuls of batter into the skillet and cook until the pancake surface begins to dry out, about 3 minutes. Flip pancakes over and cook about 2 minutes longer or until golden. Repeat with remaining batter, adding butter as needed. As pancakes are done, transfer them to a 225° oven to keep warm.

Combine the wine, remaining teaspoon of salt, and the saffron infusion in the skillet. Bring to boil over high heat and cook for 2 minutes. Add cream. Cook until liquid is reduced and thick enough to coat the back of a spoon. Add salmon and bell pepper. Cover and cook 1 to 2 minutes more, or until done. Remove from heat. Whisk in the remaining ¼ **cup** butter.

To serve, arrange endive leaves on a warm platter. Place pancakes on top. Pour salmon–red pepper sauce over.

PENNSYLVANIA DUTCH
SAFFRON BREAD

Amongst the earliest saffron users and cultivators in America were the Pennsylvania Dutch (a corruption of *Deutsch*), a sect escaping religious persecution in Germany in the 18th century. They settled in Lancaster County where each year the Folk Life Society stages a midsummer fair rich with the aroma of saffron breads and creamy sauced chicken saffron pies. I thank Ellen Szita, the author of *Wild About Saffron* for this recipe. Ellen says this is a wonderful lunch or dinner bread with hearty fare. It's lovely toasted for breakfast, and makes great breadcrumbs and chicken sandwiches.

125 saffron filaments, or	2 packets active dry yeast
3 packets powdered saffron	¼ cup lukewarm water
1 cup milk	3 large eggs
½ cup butter, cut into pieces	3 tablespoons grated lemon peel
⅓ cup sugar	3 cups all-purpose flour
1 teaspoon salt	¼ cup cornmeal

Toast the saffron filaments in a heavy pan over low heat for 1 minute, and then pound them into a fine powder in a mortar or grind with the back of a metal spoon.

Scald the milk, then add the butter, saffron, sugar, and salt. Combine, then leave to cool.

Cover the yeast with lukewarm water and a pinch of sugar, and let it rest until it foams.

Beat the eggs slightly and combine with the grated lemon peel.

In a large bowl, combine the yeast, eggs, and the milk-saffron mixture and mix well. Sift the flour and the cornmeal together and then add the milk mixture to form a soft dough. Cover the bowl with a warm towel and leave to rise for about 1 hour, or until it has doubled in size.

Punch down the dough and shape it to fit into a large loaf pan. Whisk together the egg white and water. Brush the loaf with egg wash or melted butter, and leave it to rise again to the top of the pan. Preheat the oven to 375°.

Bake the bread for 35 to 45 minutes. Cool in the pan for 10 minutes then invert onto a cooling rack.

SAFFRON MARTINI
AND OTHER TALES

AN EXAMINATION of the world of alcoholic aperitifs and digestifs reveals other facets of saffon's versatility. Four world-famous brands are blended with saffron, as a flavoring agent, as a colorant and for its restorative properties. The digestifs are based on ancient and often secret formulae, but their development as commercial brands of the modern era dates from 1840 for Yellow Chartreuse, 1845 for Fernet Branca, and 1863 for Bénédictine; the aperitif Noilly Prat was first sold in 1843.

However, saffron's use in the preparation of alcoholic beverages can be traced to many centuries before the introduction of distillation into Europe. In classical Greece in the 5th century B.C. Hippocrates described a cordial, similar to a tonic wine. It was made with saffon and various other plant extracts, including absinthe or wormwood, from which the word vermouth would later be derived. Hippocrates, "the father of modern medicine," also prescribed saffron as a means to prevent intoxication and as a hangover cure.

Absinthium Romanum was the Latin name given to a similar drink enjoyed by Apicius in Rome, five centuries later. His "Roman vermouth" was a wine-based aperitif in which saffron, wormwood, spikenard, costmary, and mastic were steeped for several days. Apicius also served a mulled wine known as *Conditum Paradoxum*, or spiced wine. A large quantity of honey was boiled down with a little wine. The aromatics were added, saffron, pepper, cinnamon, and chopped dates. More wine would then be added and the mixture simmered for an hour or more. It could be served hot or cold depending on the season.

Noilly Prat is the original dry "French Vermouth"; it is amber colored with a subtle herbal nose and a complex depth of flavor. Louis Noilly, a perfumer (who had worked with the Carthusian monks in the development of chartreuse), spent many years perfecting the precise blend and method of combining his native Herault wines with a variety of 19 different herbs and spices, which include thyme, lavender, rosemary, camomile, elder, wormwood, oregano, nutmeg, quinne, lemon balm, iris roots, and saffron.

Noilly joined in partnership with an Englishman, Claudis Prat, who then married Noilly's daughter, Marie. Together they marketed their unique vermouth to local wine merchants, then to the cafes of Paris and, via the port of Marseille, to the entire world. Noilly Prat was to become the original vermouth used in the making of the classic dry martini cocktail.

In 1510 at the Fecamp Abbey in Northern France, a monk named Bernado Vincelli, an expert in distillation and plant medicine, formulated the recipe for DOM Bénédictine. For the first time he was able to blend spices and fruits from the New World with those of the Old. His elixir combined 27 different spice and plant species, including saffron, currently supplied by Greece. Caramel, honey, and saffron are added during the final blending of Bénédictine, to harmonize the color, bouquet, and sweetness. Similarly saffron is an ingredient of B&B, the combination of Bénédictine and Brandy (cognac) which was introduced in 1937. The French Revolution, in 1789, followed by Napoleon's rule led to the dispersal of the monks, and production of Bénédictine was suspended for 70 years, until a Fecamp wine merchant rediscovered the formula and resumed supply.

The French Revolution also interrupted the distillation of chartreuse. A formula for an "elixir for long life" was passed to an order of Carthusian monks by Marshall d'Estrees in 1605. The formulation of the 130 herbs and spices was perfected in 1737 by brother Jerome Maubec, and production of the Herbal Elixir of the Grande Chartreuse began.

Swirl a measure of Fernet Branca in a brandy balloon; see how the dark brown of the bitters reveals spectacular yellow highlights and rim color. The Fratelli Branca distillery in Milan are large consumers of saffron, used in the preparation of their uniquely flavored bitters digestif, known for its recuperative properties and particularly as a hangover cure. Could it be that the original formulation of Fernet Branca included saffron for its medicinal benefits, other than just to color the final blend?

In Russia "Shafrannaya" is often prepared at home; 50 saffron filaments are infused in a bottle of vodka for a day before serving. I make my own version with a package of saffron powder. I put a little vodka into a pan on a low heat, add the saffron, and cook together for two minutes. I allow it to cool, then return the infusion to the bottle of vodka, give it a shake, and place it in the freezer. I serve it neat, in iced glasses straight from the freezer. Saffron vodka is particularly good with raw fish starters, such as oysters, smoked salmon, sushi, or caviar. The other white spirits, gin, rum and tequila, together with the clear eau de vie, can similarly be "endored" with saffron. A tiny amount will color $\frac{1}{10}$ of a gram or 1 package will flavor the spirit.

My most successful 'home brew' with saffron was as a result of a trip to Prague in the Czech Republic. I returned to London with a bottle of Becherovka, a clean, white grain spirit flavored with cinnamon. I could not resist the chance to add saffron powder to this excellent distillate, to combine with and enhance the cinnamon flavor. I like to serve my "golden" Becherovka ice cold with desserts.

The ritual making of the classic martini cocktail can be refined by the inclusion of saffron in either the gin or vodka. I developed this variation with Paco, a bartender of a Parador hotel, during the 1993 saffron harvest in La Mancha. I had in my pocket some of that morning's crop of freshly dried saffron filaments, so about $\frac{1}{20}$ of a gram was infused in a large measure of Larios gin for five minutes. Paco substituted a drop of Manzanilla sherry for the more usual dry vermouth, then he stirred the golden mixture over plenty of ice. The newly created Mancha Martini was served straight up in a cocktail glass with a single saffron filament replacing the usual olive.

I have recently discovered the charm of using vermouth instead of wine in sauces, stock, and marinades. A little saffron in the vermouth seems to lift the herbal flavor to new heights, especially in a bouillon for poaching fish. I prefer to use Chambrey vermouth from the French Alps for this purpose; it is worth seeking out, it is also a delicious drink.

Saffron ice cubes can be found in long summer drinks I serve at home. I make a saffron infusion with a kettle full of hot water, which I then allow to cool before pouring into ice trays and freezing. I always suspend a filament or two in each cube. I have also used saffron ice cubes in the two chilled summer soups of Spain: Ajo Blanco, which is from Malaga, and Gazpacho.

APPENDIX I
THE FEEL GOOD SPICE

Many cookbook writers warn of a medicinal flavor if too much saffron is used in a recipe. I wonder if they realize the prodigiousness of their remarks, as research published in the 1990s suggests that saffron could be effective in the prevention and treatment of certain cancers and tumors.

Saffron is biologically active; when ingested in moderate quantities as in most culinary applications, it has a beneficial effect on the metabolism. It has long been thought of as empathetic to the human condition and is in fact one of our oldest medicinal aids, self–regulating in dosage because of its bitterness and intensity of flavor and because of its preciousness as a resource.

The last point is just as well, as excessive dosage can prove to be toxic. Saffron is defined as a drug or narcotic in several medical references. The delicate tracery of the filaments contain an unexpected natural potency that man has respected and found therapeutic in moderation, since the birth of medical wisdom. A little goes a long way. A potentially injurious amount is said by different sources to be between 1 and 2.5 grams. The toxic symptoms of such a massive dose are *epistaxis* (nosebleed), *vertigo, vomiting* and *bradycardia* (slowing of the heart rate). Historically, saffron has also been prescribed to relieve menstrual cramps by a number of disciplines and as an aid to fertility and love making. In Indian folk medicine a weak saffon-milk infusion drunk daily by pregnant women is said to improve the complexion of the child. Also, saffron is used as a gargle by some opera singers to relax the throat before a performance.

When saffron is taken directly, as a medicine, usually in a small infusion, the dose is always small. Culpeper, in his *Complete Herbal* of the 17th century states "not more than 10 grains must be given at any one time." A grain is the equivalent of 27 saffron filaments. Therefore, the absolute maximum dose he would permit is 270 filaments, a little over half of 1 gram. While extolling the many virtues of saffron, Culpeper gave the following advice, "The use of it ought to be moderate and seasonable for when the dose is too large it produces a heaviness in the head and sleepiness, some have fallen into immoderate laughter which has ended in death." In the Victorian *Language of Flowers* saffron's name means "beware of excess."

That said, saffron's remedial properties have been recognized in the extensive literature of virtually every medical discipline worldwide for many thousands of years. Often at the heart of mainstream medical practice of the time, or as a folk remedy, it has been used to treat a vast range of illness and disease. Its use as a medicament in Britain and the USA has slowly declined in the last two hundred years, but it was until very recently to be found in the *Pharmacopoeias* of Argentina, Australia, Belgium, France, Germany, Japan, Mexico, the Netherlands, Portugal, Romania, Spain, Switzerland, and most conspicuously, in India.

At various times in history, saffron's efficacy as a curative has been viewed with suspicion and awe (at times of plague), when it was seen to possess almost magical properties that could allay many ills. For many centuries, many cultures believed saffron to be the ultimate antidote for treating poisons and the bites of venomous animals; because of the purity of its source, and its natural virtues, unsullied, almost sacramental.

Our predecessors were not to know the precise reasons for saffron's efficacy as a prescribed medicine, they could however observe the positive results of treatment with it. Color association led them to use saffron to counteract the "yellow diseases" such as jaundice and malaria.

The advances made by analytical research in only the last 70 years have revealed the complexity of saffron's nutritional web, which far exceeds the normal definition of something known as mere spice. It is the spice of life perhaps. Saffron has been found to contain so many nourishing components it could be refined as a food or as a supplement.

Analysis reveals that saffron is a particularly rich source of vitamin B_2, *riboflavin,* and has smaller traces of vitamins A, B, B_1, and C. B_2 was first isolated in the 1920s. It is a water soluble vitamin, stable to heat, acid, and oxidation but sensitive to alkali and when in solution, to light. A deficiency of B_2 is most noticeable in the condition of the mucous membranes, in particular the health of the eye. Symptoms of eye fatigue and strain, itching, and a burning sensitivity to bright light are linked to a lack of B₂, as is the susceptibility of cataracts. The Saxon *leech boke* of 900 A.D. describes a condition as "dimness of the eyes" one must heal it with crocus, saffron in French." This could be a coincidence, or it could be the results of long term observations that had proved saffron's value to the health of the eye, because of the then unknown B₂ content.

This is not the only reference to improved sight in the epoch-spanning medical literature concerned with saffron. The earliest records are found in the Sanskrit texts of the Indus Valley, which marks the beginnings of the *Ayurveda* system meaning "life knowledge." Good health is dependent on diet, moderate living, and herbal remedies, which include regular ingestion of saffron. It is an ancient system revised over many years and still practiced on a wide scale in India for a variety of conditions.

The great text of Egyptian medicine, the Ebers Papyrus, has reference to saffron's use as do the earliest Chinese medical records and the *materia medica* Pun Tsaou compiled in the 16th century.

In *Health and Food,* published in 1972 in the United States, H. M. Sinclair states, "Medicine arose from dietetics: the Pythagoreans (including Hippocrates) used diet to prevent and cure illness and drugs only if these failed." Saffron had a dual role and served both purposes of classical Greek medical theory. Hippocrates (famous for his oath) is agreed to be the founder of modern medicine. His knowledge and practice was extended by the Romans. Celsus, the physician, used saffron to treat cataracts, poisons, lethargy, and abdominal ailments. To the Romans saffron was a *pabulum,* a nutrient of a physical, mental, and spiritual kind.

The core of medical knowledge was then expanded by the advances of the Arab civilizations centered on the Caliphates of Damascus and Baghdad; their practices were introduced into Europe, together with the saffron crocus, by the Moors, with their conquest of Spain. The Saxon leech boke was in fact largely based on the writings of Hippocrates, by then already 700 years old. The Salerno School near Naples was a center of medical learning between the 10th and 14th centuries and wholeheartedly endorsed the use of the locally cultivated saffron of the Abruzzi, in this quote:

"Saffron arouses joy in every breast, settles the stomach, gives the liver rest."

Apothecaries' records provide further evidence, and it was claimed by Roger Bacon that saffron delayed aging. *Pharmacopoeias* of this period are sometimes entitled with the Latin *croco* indicating the use of saffron in one or more aspects of the remedies. Gerard, the 16th century English herbalist, stressed the moderate use of saffron as being good for the senses. At this time a jolly or cheerful individual was said to have 'slept in a bagge of saffron.' Was Culpeper suggesting that saffron could be an anti-depressant, when he says, "It wonderfully helps cold applications of the brain, that come without fever; melancholy and its attendants viz sadness without cause."

Culinary use of saffron was also seen as beneficial. Invalids would be enticed into eating properly by the use of saffron-infused broths which aided the recuperative process. The aroma of safranal would stimulate the appetite, and promote saliva and digestive "saps." The yet to be discovered B₂ content would also aid the digestion of fats, carbohydrates, and proteins, thereby speeding recovery by better nutrition.

Crocologia: seu curiosa croci regis vegetabilium enucleatio, announces Johann Ferdinand Hertodt (1647–1714) on the title page of his emphatic saffron treatise published in Jena, Germany in 1670. It has nearly 300 pages and 23 chapters, 14 of which are dedicated to the treatment of specific illnesses with saffron, and include: *afthma, angina, anorexia, arthritis, catarrhus, colica, impotentia ad venerem, lethargos, mania, naufea, ophthalmia, secundinae retentai, tumour, vertigo, ulcus,* and a condition known then as *affectio hypochondriaea* and many more.

Saffron and sugar steeped in brandy for several days was used as a folk remedy for the consumptive cough in England around 1700. Later, in the 18th century, Pio Font Quer declares, "Saffron is an excellent comforting tonic, fortifying the heart and the vital spirits. It is efficacious for all contagious or malignant illnesses, petechial fevers, smallpox, cures spleen and liver obstructions and also preserves the lungs, calms cough, and may also be used for respiratory problems. It is a remedy for uterus, helps facilitate pregnancies and is also an emmenagogue."

There is a record of saffron being used to cause the eruption of measles in London in the early part of the 20th century. In *The Hand Book of Medicinal Herbs* published in the United States in 1929, the author James A. Duke records the American folk remedy's tradition which combines Old and New World and the unique knowledge of the Native Americans. On saffron, he says that it is an extremely often cited remedy for various types of cancer, e.g. tumors of the abdomen, bladder, ear, eye, kidney, liver, neck, spleen, stomach,and tonsils, as well as cancers of the breast, mouth, stomach, uterus, venereal condylomata, and warts. He also says that saffron was used to help diabetics and people suffering from shock and spasms. He then lists an extremely detailed analysis of saffron's properties, but offers no explanations as to why it could be curative for any of the illnesses he mentions.

In 1970 F.K. Kasumov published *The Extract of Saffron Flowers in Baku*, a modern study of the traditional herbal/folk medicines used by the peoples of Azerbaijan for centuries. This publication aroused a greater interest to research saffron's specific therapeutic actions.

Important Medicinal Plants of Jammu and Kashmir" 1 Kesar (saffron) by T N Stivastava *et al* was published in 1985 in the *Science of Life*, the Journal of the Institute of Ayurveda. The two saffron preparations of the Ayurvedic practice are known as *Jumkumadi-Ghrita* and *Kumkum-madaya-taila*. It is prescribed in doses of between 1.5 to 3 grains (40 to 80 filaments). Saffron is considered as an aphrodisiac, astringent, cordial, deobstruent, diuretic, emmenagogue, stimulant, and stomachic. It is used to treat a variety of conditions, which include loss of appetite, asthma, catarrhal infections, children's affections, dyspepsia, diarrhea and dysentery, epilepsy, fevers, and enlargement of liver and spleen. It is given to relieve flatulent colic. Externally as a paste, it relieves headache, neuralgic pain, bruises, and superficial sores. Internally pessaries are given for infections of the uterus. It is considered helpful in curing anemia and for infections of the urinary tract and kidney. It cures cholera. It is a general tonic and is a good stimulant to heart, brain, liver, and sex.

At the Institute of Botany in Baku during the 1980s, Fikrat Abdullaev conducted further experiments with saffron extract. His interest was the possibility of an inhibiting effect and of saffron's curative potential in cases of cancer and tumor. In 1991, as a result of an exchange program between the Academics of Sciences in the United States and the former Soviet Union, Dr. Abdullaev traveled to Rutgers University in New Jersey to further his research. He joined with Gerald Frinkel and his team at the Department of Biological Sciences. The two doctors published three papers in the English scientific journal *Bio Factors* in 1992–93 and quote from other papers, particularly Salomi and Nair, also published in the 1990s with their research into a curative effect of saffron in cases of cancer.

Abdullaev and Frinkel describe the background to their research:"to evaluate the effectiveness of some naturally occurring constituents of food in the prevention of cancer and the relationship between the ingestion of carotenoid contained in fruits and vegetables and the risk of certain forms of cancer."Their first paper, *Bio Factors* vo.l. 3, no. 3, is the result of their initial investigations into saffron's ability to prevent the cancer cells from forming colonies and proliferating. They recorded a 50% inhibition rate at 2 hours and 90% at 5 hours on cancer cells in test tubes. A greater inhibitory effect was also noted if cells were treated with saffron prior to seeding with the various cancers.

They conclude by saying that, "the pharmacological bases of saffron are unknown, studies are currently in progress to identify the active compound(s) in saffron extract and to define their mode of action.""Saffron extracts have previously been shown to contain many compounds including carotenoids such as crocin and crocetin, which are believed to exert a toxic effect on tumor cells."They also note that, "safety (of saffron) has been effectively demonstrated by frequent consumption by large numbers of people over long periods of time."

In their second paper (vol. 4 no. 1), they state that, "over 600 potential chemopreventive agents have been identified and some of these might be utilized as anticancer drugs in the future.""Saffron extract has been shown to significantly prolong the lifespan of tumor-bearing mice, including those with sarcoma 180, Ehrlich ascites carcinoma, and Dalton's lymphoma ascites tumors.""It has also been shown to inhibit chemically induced carcinogenesis and the growth of transplanted tumors."They also say that its widespread use in food indicates that it is likely to possess relatively low toxicity. It is interesting in this regard that the saffron extract has also been shown to ameliorate some of the toxic side effects of cisplatin and cyclophosphamide, widely used chemotherapeutic agents. (Nair *et al* 1991).

Dr. Abdullaev is the author of the third paper, *The Biological Effects of Saffron, Bio Factors* vol. 5 no. 2. In it, he reviews all the literature concerning the biological activities of saffron, pointing out the numerous studies that have now revealed that it possesses cytotoxic, anticarcinogenic and antitumor properties in laboratory experiments. The possible mechanism of saffron's action, he says, is as yet poorly understood. The most consistent observation regarding saffron's mode of action has been its inhibiting effect on nucleic acid (the agent that transfers the genetic code) of tumor cells and on the cells' protein synthesis. He also states that in another study, saffon was shown to have an inhibitory effect on skin carcinogenesis in mice, by topical application. It delayed the onset and reduced the number of papillomas per animal.

He also adds, interestingly, that it is important to note that the anti-tumor effect of various spice extracts could be demonstrated only when there was oral ingestion of it, not by injection. This indicated that a prior metabolism of the ingredients in spices may be needed for their anti-tumor activity. This is known as an adaptagentic agent. He lists other spices that have been found to have chemopreventive properties on different cancers and tumors; they include: asafoetida, black pepper, black cumin, garlic, ginger, mustard, rosemary, selenium, turmeric, black and green tea, and wasabi.

He concludes, "although more studies are needed to determine the exact mechanism of their action, natural extracts provide some of the most original and promising approaches for discovery of new drugs which will have an antitumor action." As will a diverse and varied diet that contains plenty of fresh fruits and vegetables, herbs and spices.

The Amala Cancer Research Centre in Trichor Kerala, India also published papers in 1991–92 on the antitumor and antioxidant properties of saffron. Other modern studies have suggested that saffron is a beneficial agent in reducing the incidence or severity of atherosclerosis. It has been observed that where consumption of saffron is high there is less cardiovascular disease; other dietary factors need also to be considered in these findings. Saffron action in such cases is to increase oxygen diffusion in plasma, preventing hypoxia at the vascular wall (hypoxia can cause the chest pain known as *angina pectoris*). Very few compounds have such an action; crocetin has been found to bring about an 80% increase in the oxygen diffusivity of plasma. It has also been found that crocetin will reduce cholesterol and triglyceride levels in rabbits. In 1991 the Pasteur Institute reported on experiments they had conducted in Madagascar, where saffron was found to inhibit the *helicobacter pylori* infection, related to the incidence of peptic ulcers.

Modern medical patents are still being issued which record the diversity of saffron's remedial applications: as a treatment for skin papillomas, for spinal cord injuries, to treat hypertension, and in dental preparations. Saffron is patented in a further agent that increases fermentation yields. The corm (bulb) of *crocus sativus*, which is toxic, has not escaped the examination of researchers. In Australia, an extract of the corm is sold in a patented product to restore hair loss. In India, a paste is made from the ground corms and milk for external application in cases of rheumatoid arthritis.

I have been surprised to discover such an extensive wealth of knowledge and application of saffron's medicinal properties. Its use by so many differing medical disciplines to treat a wide range of corresponding conditions indicates a commonly realised efficacy too obvious to ignore or disregard. Saffron's everyday use as a medicine in the West has declined. However, the ongoing research possibly heralds a return of saffron to the forefront of medical science, as part of the curative process for some of the modern world's most grievous afflictions.

It is as a preventive that saffron may exert its most benign influence. By maintaining good health and purging the body of germs or disease, before the illness can establish itself, it is described as an antiseptic or as an antibacterial in several references. Is it too simplistic to suggest that regular and moderate culinary use of a natural product, saffron, would help to procure equilibrium within the system because of its diverse nutritive composition.

Consider saffron's domain; could it be that the delicate filaments are a potent and vital ingredient of the famed Mediterranean diet that has been overlooked in the rush to the shops for olive oil and garlic? If saffron is used with the knowledge that it aids good digestion, it is a benefit enjoyed. That it may be doing some other good at a deeper level is further encouragement. The classical world believed saffron promoted longevity, and Francis Bacon (1561–1626) had this to say: "The English are rendered sprightly by a liberal use of saffron in sweetmeats and broths."

APPENDIX II
SAFINTER S.A. BARCELONA

The tram station for the Tibidabo marks the boundary between the city blocks and the spacious avenues of Modernista architecture. I always notice a change in the air as I walk past, up the hill, to Safinter's elegant headquarters in the north of Barcelona, my favorite city.

It is a vital city because of its strategic position, its history of commerce, and its access to foreign markets. These are some of the good reasons Luis González had for moving the family business from Albacete (La Mancha) to the Catalan capital in 1958. He also wanted to gain a better location for the export trade he had developed since joining his father, Valeriano González, who founded the company in 1912.

Having completed his commercial and business studies, Luis pursued his vocation to increase the world market for the company's top-quality Mancha saffron. In 1951 he exhibited at a trade show in Karachi, and then traveled for three months to all the major cities in India and other Asian countries.

The expansion of the business provided funds for inward investment. New laboratory instruments were purchased and qualified technical staff hired. As quality control has been vital in the continuing success of the company, modern packaging equipment has allowed new products to be developed for the retail market.

In 1982 Safinter S.A. was established as a continuation of Valeriano's company. Luis was joined by the third generation, his daughters Luz and Isobell. They brought new energy and marketing skills to the business, ensuring that the company's brands, Safinter and Taj Mahal, enjoyed the highest reputation in the world.

Each autumn the old house in Albacete is opened up, and becomes a saffron gathering center. Meanwhile the family roam across the plain purchasing only the highest qualities directly from the growers. Grading, sorting, analyzing, packaging, and dispatch are all undertaken in Barcelona.

Safinter have export clients in Italy, Sweden, Switzerland, Norway, England, the United Arab Emirates and other Gulf states, Singapore, Malaysia, Japan, Hong Kong, and the United States of America.

In 1989 Safitalia was incorporated to promote Safinter's products in Italy under a Spanish trademark and control.

More recently, in cooperation with the International Standards Organization (ISO) of Geneva, Safinter has been instrumental in the formation of Norme, ISO 3632-1/21/8 1993, a test system to determine the quality of saffron by analysis, which is accurate, repeatable, and easy. Taking just two hours with the correct equipment, a 10-gram sample of saffron is needed, split 2 x 5 gram, so it is possible to duplicate the tests. This has now become the international standard for saffron, accepted by the European Union and the saffron industry.

The ISO has kindly allowed me to reproduce table 2-ISO 3632-1 chemical requirements for saffron (see Appendix III).

Safinter's dedication to quality and sheer enthusiasm for their product has been a great assistance to me in the writing of this book, for which I am very grateful.

APPENDIX III

The International Organization for Standardization (ISO), Geneva, Switzerland published its International Standard No ISO 3632 - 1 and 2 in 1993.

They are titled:

Saffron (*Crocus Sativus Linnaeus*)

Part 1   Specification
Part 2   Test Methods

© International Standard ISO 3632 1 was prepared by Technical Committee ISO/TC 34, Agricultural food products - Sub Committee S.C.7 - Spices and Condiments.

The first edition of ISO 3632-1 together with ISO 3632-2 cancels and replaces ISO 3632 - 1980 of which they constitute a technical revision.

The ISO have kindly given me permission to reproduce ISO 3632-1 1993 E table 2 page 4 and Section 8. Packing and marking from the same standard.

Chemical requirements for saffron, in filaments or in powder form

Requirement

Characteristic	saffron in filaments	saffron in powder form	Test Method
Moisture and volatile matter % (m/m), max	12	10	ISO 3632-2, clause 9
Total ash, % (m/m), on dry basis, max	8	8	ISO 928 and ISO 3632-2, clause 10
Acid-insoluble ash, % (m/m), on dry basis, max Categories I and II	1,0	1,0	ISO 930 and
Categories III and IV	1,5	1,5	ISO 3632-2 clause 11
Solubility in cold water,'% (m/m), on dry basis, max	65	65	ISO 941
Bitterness, expressed as direct of the absorbance of reading picrocrocine at about 257nm, on dry basis, min			
Category I	70	70	
Category II	55	55	ISO 3632-2,
Category III	40	40	clause 3
Category IV	30	30	
Safranal, expressed as direct reading of the absorbance at about 330nm, on dry basis All categories			ISO 3632-2,
min	20	20	clause 13
max	50	50	

Coloring strength, expressed as direct reading of the absorbance of crocine at about 440nm, on dry basis, min			
Category I	190	190	ISO 3632-2, clause 13
Category II	150	150	
Category III	110	110	
Category IV	80	80	
Total nitrogen, % (m/m), on dry basis, max [1]	3,0	3,0	ISO 1871
Crude fiber, % (m/m), on dry basis, max [1]	6	6	ISO 5498

[1] Additional tests which may be carried out if necessary, if sufficient sample is available.

APPENDIX IV

USEFUL CONTACTS

Saffron Merchants

Bacstrom Imports Company
P.O. Box 8262
Emeryville, CA 94662
510–658–9713

Penzeys Ltd. Spice House
P.O. Box 1448
Waukesha, WI 53187
414–574–0277

Saffron Direct
Suite 23, 46-48 Warwick Way
London SW1V 1RY
send sase for price list, trade and private customers

Saffron Imports
949 Valencia Street
San Francisco, CA 94110
415–648–8990

Suppliers of Saffron Corms (Bulbs)

Saffron Walden Museum
Museum Street, Saffron Walden
Essex CB10 1JL Tel: 01799 510333

Poyntzfield Herb Nursery
Black Isle by Dingwall, IV7 8LX
Ross & Cromarty, Scotland
Tel: 01381 610352
send 3 first class stamps and addressed envelope for mail order catalogue.

Blackdown Lilies
Venn Ottery, Exeter, Devon
Tel: 01395 567605

Cornish Bakers with postal cake service

W. T. Warren & Son
Bosweddon Road, St Just, Penzance
Cornwall, TR19 7JU
Tel: 01736 788538

Blewetts of Truro
Malpas Road, Truro, Cornwall TR1 1QH
Tel: 01872 72069

Couch's
Lawn Bakery, St. Blazey
Par Cornwall, PL24 2NW
Tel: 01726 812358

Many of the recipes in this book were made with produce purchased from The Tachbrook Street market in Pimlico, London SW1. I take this opportunity to thank the following traders: Ivano Delicatessen and Ivano Greengrocer, Bonne Bouche the baker, Harts of Victoria the butcher; Rippon Cheese Stores, Holland and Barrett, and Gastronomia Italia. Also in nearby Warwick Way, SW1, La Bella Sicilia, Oddbins and Tesco.

BIBLIOGRAPHY

Andrews, Colman. *Catalan Cuisine.* London: Headline, 1986.

Annand, Kenneth Fraser and Butener, Ann. *A Taste of Cornwall, Recipes and Ramblings.* Tredinnick Press, 1994.

Aryan, J R and Aryan, R.D. *Botany of Saffron.* 1970.

Aucante, Pierra. *Saveurs du Safron.* Albin Michel, 1993.

Aziz, Khalid. *Indian Cookery.* London: Hamlyn, 1974.

Bio Factors, Vol. 3 No. 3 1992, Vol. 4 No. 1 1992, Vol. 4 No. 2 Oxford University Press (now published by IOS Press, Amsterdam) 1993.

Bissell, Frances. *The Times Cook Book.* Chatto & Windus, 1993.

Bowles, E.A. *A Handful of Crocus and Colchicum.* Bodley Head, 1924 and 1952.

Bowring, K.N.M. *Around the Fal.* Exeter University

Carluccio, Antonio. *An Invitation to Italian Cooking.* London: Pavilion, 1986.

Carter, Elizabeth. *Majorcan Food.* Prospect Books, 1989.

Casas, Penelope. *The Foods and Wines of Spain.* London: Penguin, 1979.

CIBA *Review* No. 1

Clarke FSA, Joseph. *Notes on the Saffron Plant.* London: The Pharmaceutical Journal, 1887.

Colin, Jane. *Herbs and Spices.* Arlington Books, 1989.

Coppock, Heather. *The Saffron Crocus in Cherry Hinton and other areas* of *Cambridgeshire.* 1984

Cornish Cookery. Conran Octopus, 1993.

Cornwall Federation of Women's Institutes. *What's Cooking in Cornwall.*

Cromarty, Dorothy. *Fields of Saffron*

Crookes, William. *Handbook of Dyeing and Calico Printing.* Longmans Green & Co, 1874.

Culpeper's *Complete Herbal.* W Foulsham & Co. Ltd.

David, Elizabeth. *Spices, Salt and Aromatics in the English Kitchen.* London: Penguin, 1970.

Duke, James A. *Handbook of Medicinal Herbs.* Florida: CRC Press, 1929.

Evans, Mark. *Herbal Plants,* Studio Editions, London 1991

Evans, Maureen. *Saffron Walden.* Local History Activity Guide, 1992.

Falaise, Maxime de la. *Seven Centuries of English Cooking.* Grove Press, 1973.

Fancett, William. *Saffron Walden Parish Church*

Gerarde, J. *The Herbal or General History of Plants.* London, 1597.

Giró, Joseph Lladonosai. *El Libre de la Cocina Catalana.* Madrid: Alianza Editorial.

Goldstein, Darra. *A Taste of Russia (A La Russe).* Harper Perennial, 1991.

Goodwin, Jill. *A Dyers Manual.* London: Pelham Books, 1982.

Griffin, Richard, 3rd Lord Braybrooke. *The History of Audley End.* Samuel Bentley, 1836.

Halicis, Nevin. *Turkish Cookbook.* London: Dorling Kindersley, 1989.

Hawke, Kathleen. *A Cornish Hotchpotch.* Cornwall: Dyllansow Truran, 1989.

Heard, Vida. *Recipes of Today and Yesteryear.* Cornwall: Dyllansow Truran, 1984.

Hertodt, J.F. *Crocologia.* Germany: Jena, 1670.

Hirsh, Jennifer. *The Saffron Crocus.* Saffron Walden Museum, Leaflet No 13.

Hill MD, John. *Doctor Hill's Family Herbal,* 2nd Edition. 1755.

Kasumov, F.J. *The Extract of Saffron Flowers*. Baku: Gos Plan Press, 1970.

Little, Alastair and Whittington, Richard. *Keep it Simple.* Conran Octopus, 1994.

Martin, Carolyn. *Our Daily Bread, Secrets from the Bakers of Cornwall.* Tabb House, 1993.

Martindale Pharmacopoeia, 30th edition.

Matthew, Brian. *The Crocus.* London: B T Batsford, 1982.

Maw, George. *A Monograph of the Genus Crocus.* London: Dulva & Co., 1886.

Miller, Philip. *Gardeners Dictionary.* 1731.

Mitchell, Rynbergen, Anderson and Dibble. *Nutrition in Health and Disease*, 16th edition. New York: J B Lippincott, 1976.

Mulherin, Jennifer. *Spices and Natural Flavorings.* London: Tiger Books, 1992.

Norman, Jill. *The Complete Book of Spices.* London: Dorling Kindersley, 1986.

Okakangas, Beatrice - *The Great Scandinavian Baking Book.* Canada Little Brown and Company,, 1988.

Pandey, B.P. *Spices and Condiments.* New Delhi, India: Shree Publishing, 1990.

Pellowe, Susan. *Saffron and Currants.* Aurora: Renard Productions, 1989.

Reejhsunghani, Aroona. *The Great Art of Mughlai Cooking.* New Dehli: Vikas Publishing House, 1979.

Rees, A.R. *Saffron - An Expensive Plant Product.* London: Home and Law Publishing.

Richardson, Rosamond. *Exotic Spices.* London: Piatkus, 1985.

Ruksans, Janis. *Krokusi.* Avots, 1981.

Saffron Walden 1236. 1986, Official Brochure, Charter 750, Saffron Walden 1985.

Samat, Maguelonne Toussaint. *History of Food.* Blackwells Publishers, 1987.

Scater, J.W. *Manual of Colors & Dye Wares.* Lockwood and Co., 1870.

Scott, David. *Grains, Beans and Nuts.* London: Hutchinson, 1986.

Shaida, Margaret. *The Legendary Cuisine of Persia.* London: Lieuse Publications, 1992.

Singh, Digvijaya. *Cooking Delights of the Maharajas.*, Bombay: Vakils, Feffer Simons, 1982.

Solomon, Charmaine. *The Complete Asian Cookbook.* London: Grub Street, 1976.

Srivastava, T N, Rajasekharan, S, Badola, D P, Shah, D C. *Ancient Science of Life.* India: The Journal of International Institute of Ayurveda Vol. V No. 1, 1985.

Strang, Jeanne. *Goose Fat and Garlic.* London: Kyle Cathie, 1991.

Style, Sue. *A Taste of Switzerland.* New York: Hearst Books.

Swahn, J.O. *The Lore of Spices.* Sweden: AB Nordbok.

Szita, Ellen. *Wild About Saffron.* Saffron Rose, 1987.

Tannahill, Realy. *Food in History.* London: Penguin, 1973 and 1988

The British Medical Association. *Complete Family Health.* London: Dorling Kindersley, 1990.

The Lawrence Review of Natural Products. St Louis: J B Lippincott

The Plants Man, Vol. 9-10, 1987-9.

The Women's Fellowship of the Methodist Church (Cornwall). *Family Favourites.*

Vijay, G Padma. *Indian and Mughlai Rice Treats.* New Dehli: Sterling Paperbacks, 1992.

Walker, Jane. *Creative Cooking with Spices.* London: Tiger Books, 1986.

Wilson, C Anne. *Food and Drink in Britain.* London: Constable & Co, 1973.

Wirth and Gatherceal. *Pharmacognosy.* Philadelphia: Lea and Gebiger, 1947.

Warburg, E.F. *Crocuses.* Endeavour Vol. XVI, 1957.

INDEX
Recipes